Internet-Delivered CBT

Internet-Delivered CBT: Distinctive Features offers a concise overview of how internet-delivered CBT and related methods (such as smartphones) can be used as single interventions as well as part of regular CBT in the form of "blended treatments". The book also describes different applications and adaptions of internet treatments for different target groups (young persons, adults and older adults) and cultures/languages.

The book is in the style of A–Z, which means that all stages will be described from assessment/case formulation, treatment and how clinicians can/should support the treatments, evaluations and also new findings regarding the role of tailoring treatments based on client problem profile and preferences.

The book is written for clinical psychologists, psychotherapists and also students in these fields. It is also suitable for researchers in the field of digital treatments.

Gerhard Andersson is a full professor in clinical psychology and a world leading researcher in the field of internet-delivered psychological treatments. He has published many studies and books and is among the most cited researchers in clinical psychology in the world. He is also a trained CBT psychotherapist and practises as a clinical psychologist.

T0384910

CBT Distinctive Features
Series Editor: Windy Dryden

Cognitive behaviour therapy (CBT) occupies a central position in the move towards evidence-based practice and is frequently used in the clinical environment. Yet there is no one universal approach to CBT and clinicians speak of first-, second-, and even third-wave approaches.

This series provides straightforward, accessible guides to a number of CBT methods, clarifying the distinctive features of each approach. The series editor, Windy Dryden successfully brings together experts from each discipline to summarise the 30 main aspects of their approach divided into theoretical and practical features.

The CBT Distinctive Features Series will be essential reading for psychotherapists, counsellors, and psychologists of all orientations who want to learn more about the range of new and developing cognitive behaviour approaches.

Recent titles in the series:

Internet-Delivered CBT: Distinctive Features by Gerhard Andersson

Single-Session Integrated CBT: Distinctive features, 2nd Edition by Windy Dryden

Beck's Cognitive Therapy: Distinctive Features, 2nd Edition by Frank Wills

Rational Emotive Behaviour Therapy: Distinctive Features, 3rd Edition by Windy Dryden

Integrating CBT and 'Third Wave' Therapies by Dr Fiona Kennedy and Dr David Pearson

Motivational Cognitive Behavioural Therapy by Cathy Atkinson, Paul Earnshaw

For further information about this series please visit www.routledge.com/ CBT-Distinctive-Features/book-series/DFS

Internet-Delivered CBT

Distinctive Features

Gerhard Andersson

Routledge
Taylor & Francis Group

LONDON AND NEW YORK

First published 2025
by Routledge
4 Park Square, Milton Park, Abingdon, Oxon OX14 4RN

and by Routledge
605 Third Avenue, New York, NY 10158

Routledge is an imprint of the Taylor & Francis Group, an informa business

© 2025 Gerhard Andersson

British Library Cataloguing-in-Publication Data
A catalogue record for this book is available from the British Library

ISBN: 978-1-032-59193-3 (hbk)
ISBN: 978-1-032-59192-6 (pbk)
ISBN: 978-1-003-45344-4 (ebk)

DOI: 10.4324/9781003453444

Typeset in Times New Roman
by Apex CoVantage, LLC

Contents

Figures and tables

Figures

Tables

Part I

BACKGROUND, TECHNIQUES AND ASSUMPTIONS

1

Introduction

Psychotherapy is sometimes called the "talking cure", but cognitive behaviour therapists have since the start relied on complementary ways to obtain change for their clients, including sheets with instructions on how to do homework, use of video or audio recordings and informative texts, just to give a few examples. The format of cognitive behaviour therapy (CBT) has also varied from the start, including the traditional one-to-one face-to-face format, group CBT, couples therapy, family therapy, and, not the least, self-help CBT in various versions. I began my research and clinical career in the field of behavioural medicine/health psychology working only with paper-and-pencil questionnaires, face-to-face and group treatment delivery in a world in which the main way to get new information was to go to the library as few people had computers at home and the internet was not around. One generation back, researchers did not usually even have access to computers, and one major step had already occurred when I began my PhD study as data management and writing text using computers was a major advancement which preceded the internet. A second technological advancement came with first the mobile phones, and then in the early 2010s smartphones which, in retrospect, may be the most influential change in society as we not only have access to the internet at home and work but have it everywhere with our smartphones. It is almost hard to imagine how much the world has changed now almost 30 years later when the internet and modern information technology is everywhere and in the hands of a majority of people in the world given smartphone access. It was estimated

DOI: 10.4324/9781003453444-2

that in 2023, as many as 68% of the world's population had access to the internet. In Europe and United States (and closely followed by Latin America and Middle East) it is estimated that about nine out of 10 persons have internet access (*https://internetworldstats.com/*). Some regions still lag a bit behind, but it is still amazing that so many persons in the world can connect, seek information and take advantage of the speed in which news can travel via the internet. Some readers probably right now think about the problems as well. Of course the world is far from perfect with limited internet access, blocked information, false information including internet bubbles, tracking persons without consent, marketing, abuse, internet addiction and many other cons which makes the internet problematic sometimes. When I write this we have just left a pandemic (Covid-19), which was earlier described as a "Black Swan" for mental health and e-health (Wind et al., 2020). We have now entered a new era in which artificial intelligence (AI) is portrayed as either a blessing or a curse, but in any case something that already has an impact and may be even more influential and change the way we use computers (including smartphones) and the internet. I will return to this matter later in the book as it is very uncertain in which ways we may benefit from AI, including how well chatbots and "artificial therapists" may be used.

Most readers will not need any introduction to what the internet is and how it works (or perhaps you are not even interested?). I will stick with the term *internet* in this book, which was not obvious with alternative terms like World Wide Web, cyberspace, the Net, online network etc. being used. Now we can just ask the computer what the internet is and get a decent AI-generated answer: "a global computer network providing a variety of information and communication facilities, consisting of interconnected networks using standardized communication protocols". The reason I mention this is that the use of the internet in CBT has suffered from a chaotic terminology which began from the start more than 20 years ago (Smoktunowicz et al., 2020). When we investigated this matter, we found inconsistent use of terms and noted that this leads to miscommunication between stakeholders including both researchers and clinicians.

Most likely also patients/clients as it can be very hard to understand if internet means video contact or a guided self-help program. During the pandemic health care contacts using video became more common and accepted, but as I will return to in this book, there is much less research on video delivery of CBT compared to self-help with or without clinical support. But returning to the terminology issue, just to give an example, when many researchers call their treatment internet-delivered CBT and use the acronym ICBT, others may instead use the term web-based CBT, online CBT, digital CBT, and it is obvious that this is not helpful in the long run as the field of psychotherapy (and CBT) already has a problem with terminology. Further, standardization is even more important when it comes to technical solutions. We proposed a glossary as a potential solution to remedy the inconsistent terminology issue (Smoktunowicz et al., 2020). Back in 2004 I took the initiative to invite researchers for an initial meeting in Stockholm, Sweden, on internet and CBT, and some of the pioneers in the field came. One of them was professor Lee Ritterband from the United States who had just published a review paper using the term "internet interventions" (Ritterband et al., 2003). During the meeting we initiated a world organization which became the International Society for Research on Internet Interventions (ISRII; www.isrii.org). About 10 years later a journal was launched with the title *Internet Interventions*, which is now one of the top journals in the field. Even if I will not manage to resolve the issue of inconsistent terminology, I will use the term internet and internet-delivered CBT (ICBT) most of the time in this book. Having said that, terms like e-health and m-health may pop up, but both of these usually involve the internet unless unconnected stand-alone solutions are used for which the broader term digital health may be more appropriate.

The scope of the book

This book will cover many aspects of how you can use the internet and modern information technology overall in CBT. I will describe how ICBT and related methods (such as smartphones) can be used as single interventions, as well as part of regular CBT in the form of "blended treatments". It is important to note already here that I see no real conflict between ICBT and regular provision of CBT in the therapy room. Indeed, I work as clinician myself and believe that it is good to have different means for different clients and also combine approaches when needed. It is also very clear that resources are scarce, and the demand for services requires that we consider different solutions including reaching clients earlier when it may be possible to prevent development of more severe problems. The book describes different applications and adaptions of ICBT for different problem areas (psychiatric conditions, somatic conditions and other target groups such as lonely persons), age groups (young persons, adults and older adults) and cultures/languages. The book is in the style of A–Z, which means that all stages will be described from assessment/case formulation, treatment and how clinicians can/should support the treatments, evaluations and also what we can learn from ICBT research. Indeed, the balance between face-to-face psychotherapy research and research on internet-delivered treatments has turned, and it is now often the case that the largest studies and newest developments in CBT are done using the internet.

2

Self-help treatments and bibliotherapy

Using text to obtain advice, support and self-help treatment has been around since we humans began to read and write. Historically, this has mostly been in the form of religious texts such as the Bible, but also in more modern times fiction/novels and self-help books (Watkins & Clum, 2008). I will focus here on self-help books knowing that the term *self-help* is complicated and often used to describe self-help support groups lead by laypersons. Self-help books have been around for a long time and have also been the focus of much research. Rosen (1987) commented on the fact that psychological self-help books are commercial products with numerous potential buyers and a dissemination that by far exceed the number of clients that can be seen in the clinic.

Gradually, self-help books became secular and contained advice for achieving wealth, social status and health. One example is the still very popular book by Dale Carnegie *How to win friends and influence people*, published as early as 1936. One problem with self-help books also noted by Rosen (1987) is the fact that there is no requirement that the books are first tested in research, and therefore they may not be effective and potentially even do some harm. The latter risk is often handled by disclaimers and recommendations to consult clinicians/health care first, but the first problem of lack of research is usually not an argument against publishing a self-help book. Another potential problem can occur when there is research support for a self-help book, but the study included support from a clinician while completing the self-help treatment described in the book. When the book is later sold in the bookstore, such support is

DOI: 10.4324/9781003453444-3

not available. The difference between guided and non-guided pure self-help is a longstanding dilemma in research and clinical practice and has been a topic of much interest in ICBT research from the very start.

One argument for CBT self-help books is often that that the treatment presented as a self-help treatment is based on a face-to-face treatment that has been tested in rigorous research trials. However, it is not obvious that a face-to-face treatment works in the self-help format, even if this often is the case when it comes to CBT. Oddly, the problem with many self-help books not being tested in research is even worse when it comes to modern self-help smartphone apps, which I will return to later in this book.

In spite of the many CBT self-help books without research support, there are several good examples of books that have been tested. Two examples when it comes to depression are *Feeling good* (Burns, 1980) and *Control your depression* (Lewinsohn et al., 1986), which have been tested many times in research trials. In my own research we decided to publish our internet treatment for social anxiety as a self-help book, but first tested if it would work in the book format (Furmark et al., 2009), and we have done the same thing publishing books on panic disorder, depression and tinnitus after we have done ICBT studies, just to give a few examples. Indeed, the support for self-help based on books with at least minimal therapist support is robust, with effects often being on par with what we have found in ICBT and face-to-face trials (Marrs, 1995), even if there are not numerous direct comparisons. In fact, ICBT research began with inspiration from self-help books, and ICBT has even been described as "net-bibliotherapy" by Marks et al. (2007). Note here the use of the term "bibliotherapy", which was the term used for many years and still is used sometimes. A problem is that the term bibliotherapy also can mean reading fiction for therapeutic purposes, and that now most research on self-help CBT is done using information technology and not books. Self-help books do have a place and in particular, given the sometimes temporary nature of digital material (for example, if an app or a website is closed down or gone out of business). Clients may benefit from saving a printed version of their self-help treatment in case they would like to return to the material and the online program/app is not around anymore.

It can be useful for the reader to know the difference between a self-help book and text material/online programs delivered via the internet. Much is common. The text material should be clear, understandable, provide a rationale, include sheets and possibly pictures, tasks/homework and follow a structure/time plan. Basically everything in a self-help book can be delivered via the internet and even the book itself as a pdf file, which is what we did when we began doing research on ICBT. We even recommended our clients to print the material. There are some advantages with internet delivery. First, we can embed questionnaires, quiz and online exercises, making the experience more interactive. Second, the interventions can more easily be tailored based on client progress and preferences. Third, and perhaps most obvious, is the use of alternative media such as videos, audio files and even links to useful resources. Finally, and as I mentioned in relation to the research on self-help books, they tend to work better if support is given on a regular basis during the treatment. In most bibliotherapy trials, this has been done using telephone (with group meetings also being used before). This is different from the immediate but still-asynchronous text-based support that is provided in ICBT. Thus one major advantage of ICBT versus bibliotherapy CBT is the way support can be given and also the interactive features including monitoring if the client deteriorates.

Reflections

The research world and the clinical world differ. I am much aware of the common use of self-help books in face-to-face CBT, with one estimate suggesting that a majority of CBT clinicians use and recommend self-help books in their clinical work (Keeley et al., 2002). We reported consistent findings in our own survey on CBT clinicians and found that recommendation of self-help books was regarded as part of CBT and also fairly often used (Bohman et al.,

2017). In fact, on reflection, it is a bit strange that text material is not standard in the provision of CBT face-to-face. We know for example that clients remember only a portion of what is said in a therapy session and sometimes even miss the crucial information. I will return to this aspect of what is remembered by clients in CBT later on in Chapter 10, but it should be put forward as an argument in favour of using self-help books as adjuncts to face-to-face therapy. I will also mention blended treatments later on as mixing formats tend to be common in clinical practice, and self-help books are the oldest and probably still the most common approach to blend other CBT delivery formats with face-to-face services, even if websites and apps also are popular.

3

Computerized CBT

Using computers in CBT has been around for a long time and preceded ICBT and the spread of the internet. Sometimes abbreviated CCBT, there is a fairly small but important literature on the effects of delivering CBT using computer programs that, back in the days, were presented on CD-ROMS or DVDs using mainly stand-alone computers or palmtops (handheld computers that existed before smartphones). Everything changed when computers became connected to the internet, and it could be argued that ICBT is a form of CCBT even if the latter term is arguably a bit obsolete and not often used now. There are, however, still new studies published using the term and testing the effects even if they tend to use online delivery. One pioneer in the work on CCBT is professor Isaac Marks, and the history and research support for CCBT is well described in the book *Hands-on- Help: Computer-aided Psychotherapy* (Marks et al., 2007). For this chapter I want to differentiate CCBT and ICBT, with the former being the treatment format that use computer programs to deliver CBT content, with *Beating the Blues*, *FearFighter* and *BTSteps* being three examples for which there is research support. Basically everything that is in CCBT can be delivered online, and modern versions (not necessarily requiring internet connection) are smartphone applications that can be very similar to the CCBT programs in terms of content. In order to facilitate the understanding of a confusing literature, I therefore reserve the term CCBT for the programs that are not delivered online.

One of the most well studied CCBT programs is *Beating the Blues*, which was originally made available on CD-ROM and jointly

DOI: 10.4324/9781003453444-4

designed and developed by Dr Judy Proudfoot and her team at the Institute of Psychiatry, Kings College, London, together with the company Ultrasis (Proudfoot et al., 2003). The program contains eight modules and covers typical CBT components for depression. It starts with a video, and then modules cover automatic thoughts, thinking errors, challenging thoughts, core beliefs and attributional style, which are the cognitive components. But there are also behavioural components that, to some extent, are tailored based on symptoms: graded exposure, task breakdown and sleep management. Effects of the program including cost-effectiveness have been reported, and it has also been recommended by the British National Institute for Health and Care Excellence – NICE (Marks et al., 2007).

Another example of CCBT is the program *FearFighter*, developed by Isaac Marks and his team (Marks et al., 2004), which also exists as an ICBT program but was originally tested as a stand-alone computer system (CCBT) for anxiety. This program has also been endorsed by NICE. The program lasts for nine weeks and includes components such as psychoeducation, goal setting, recognizing safety behaviours, exposure techniques, cognitive therapy components and monitoring of progress. It is set up as a journey with information, exercises and videos in which four actors describe their own efforts to manage their anxieties and phobias.

A third example of CCBT is the program *BTSteps* for obsessive-compulsive disorder (OCD), developed by a joint UK-USA based team. The program was innovative as it combined a manual/workbook with a computer-driven IVR (interactive voice response) system in which the clients were guided via their phones. The treatment is basically exposure and response prevention in nine steps including psychoeducation, homework, etc. Studies were conducted showing that the program worked and reduced symptoms of OCD (Greist et al., 2002).

The research on CBT delivered via palmtops is small (also referred to by Marks et al. as handheld device systems), making it mostly of historical interest even if there were a few innovative studies (Marks et al., 2007). The advantages of portable pocket-size computer systems was later confirmed by the smartphone revolution. As palmtops never became widely available, the research was mostly done on palmtops provided by the researchers. There are, however, some studies supporting the format on, for example, panic disorder (Newman et al., 1997).

Another interesting historical background that should be mentioned here is the program *Eliza*, which most likely is the first natural language processing computer program with a psychotherapy intent (at least the most well known). It was created and launched in 1967 at Massachusetts Institute of Technology by the computer scientist Joseph Weizenbaum. The program simulated a Rogerian psychotherapy interaction using a pattern matching and substitution methodology, but with the caveat that the program did not understand what was said. I will mention *Eliza* again later in this book when we discuss chatbots (including AI), as *Eliza* arguably was one of the first attempts to create a human-computer psychotherapy communication program (Epstein & Klinkenberg, 2001). Interested readers can easily do an online search for *Eliza* and test more modern versions. Interestingly, there is not much controlled research on how well *Eliza* works, but in one controlled study on older adults (Bennion et al., 2020), some benefits were reported even if *Eliza* was the control condition.

Reflections

One striking thing to consider is how dependent the field of "digital interventions" has been on technical developments, but also what the market has lead consumers to use and what consumers have decided to use. For example, it was not obvious that tablets and the presentation of iPads and similar devices would become popular. The history of CCBT was marked by replacement of CD-ROM programs to being able to download programs from the internet. Not only did the move to the internet changed the way we provide computerized treatment programs, but it had an even more widespread effect on assessment procedures with online administration of questionnaires replacing other forms of computerized assessments to a great extent. On the other hand, computerized assessments were fairly recent as well, and it is interesting to note that assessment of suicidal intent was presented as being more efficient using computerized interviews than the standard face-to-face version, in an influential study by Greist et al. (1973), which most likely increased the acceptance of computer interviews by clinicians. I will return to internet-based assessment procedures in Chapter 6. When it comes to treatment, we need to consider if the format makes any difference as the content of CCBT programs is very similar to the subsequent internet programs and even the same sometimes when the CCBT programs like *Beating the Blues* went online. The development of ICBT was much informed by the early work done by Isaac Marks and co-workers. For the handheld computers/palmtops, it is even more clear that subsequent technology replaced them and that they perhaps never became popular enough to make any difference. Smartphones have, however, had a huge impact, and this we will return to later.

4

The internet and its role in CBT

It is likely that some readers of this book will have no recollection of a time without the internet. In this chapter I will not provide a full technical description of how the internet works, but rather comment on different ways the internet is relevant for CBT and its practitioners. In my previous book written 10 years back (Andersson, 2015), the situation was different, and technology (not the least the dramatic increased use of smartphones), social media and, more recently, AI have changed the scene for us all and will continue to do so. Moreover, it is now even more common across the globe to access the internet. As I stated earlier, in 2023 it was estimated that as many as 68% of the world's population have access to the internet (www.internetworldstats.com), Disparities remain, with North America (93%) and Europe (89%) taking the lead with more or less total coverage. Then there are regions with almost as high a penetration rate such as Latin America (81%), Middle East (77%), Oceania/Australia (70%) and Asia (67%). Africa still lags behind (43%), but there the growth rate is much higher than the rest of the world. Another way to look at the statistics is where most internet users live, and not surprisingly, given the size of the population, as many as 54% of all internet users reside in Asia. But perhaps most striking to me when I revisit the statistics now is that some places in Europe like Romania have now about as many internet users as the rest of Europe, and it is remarkable how much the world has changed just the last 10 years.

Many things remain the same as in my 2015 book. People use the internet on a regular basis for information and communication, but also for business, handling money, travel bookings, dating and numerous other human activities. Briefly, the internet is a global system of computer networks that are interconnected via servers who "communicate" via shared computer languages. There are layers and different systems involved, but the internet has four layers. First, we have the link layer, which contains technologies for local network communication. Second, we have the internet layer, which connects different local networks (which was the main idea behind the internet). Third, we have something called the transport layer, where web hosts communicate (servers). Finally, at the highest level we have the application layer, which handles more specific protocols used for communication with a range of purposes. There are many other aspects I will not cover here, but it is interesting to note that while technology is more advanced and we access the internet via different devices, the World Wide Web (WWW) and websites in many ways function as they did more than 20 years back, which suggests that some form of technology standardization took place, at least from the users' point of view. This might change now with AI applications being embedded increasingly in search engines, but it may also be that consumers will prefer to have some control and that we are used to having more or less free information in many places of the world.

For now we can still assume that the internet often can be accessed via different devices (many have only smartphone access) at a fairly low cost, and that a majority of workplaces will involve at least some handling of computers that are connected to the internet. It is also the case that it is getting hard to live without a smartphone (for example, when travelling in Sweden most busses and trains will not accept cash). Further, with 5G emerging and with smartphones directly being connected to the internet, it is also the case that we are used to being able to use the internet in most places even if costs can vary. The internet is also increasingly part of our environment, which has been referred to as "the internet of things", which briefly describes how physical objects are embedded with sensors, software and other technologies (for example, sound systems for listening to music, monitoring of our homes via web cameras, cars being connected for updates of programs). This is happening fast but has already led to benefits for health care (e.g., monitoring of heart activity from a distance).

But what about the relevance of the internet for the practice of CBT? If we first start with our clients, they are likely to be internet users and therefore can search for information regarding CBT and even check you as a therapist. In Sweden it is also common that patients can access their medical files online, get reminders for appointments, etc. Not all patients use this opportunity to check their medical files, but at least it is possible. When it comes to specific patient groups, it was common before with online support groups/dedicated web pages on various topics, and they still exist but have been complemented and often even replaced with social media groups. Patient organizations also use the internet to increase awareness, and when it comes to mental health, much activity occurs online. My point here is that both clients and clinicians are affected by what is out there, and, for example, what is written about CBT in media is not only a local thing but can have widespread consequences (not necessarily negative with, for example, research news).

Second, as a practitioner, you are likely to belong to online networks related to CBT (mainly social media such as Facebook), and also to buy your books online, perhaps view a YouTube video on a therapeutic technique (which also clients may do) and attend online lectures (which showed a dramatic increase during the Covid-19 years). Then CBT clinicians also supervise and get supervision using the internet, and if you want to check recent research, many scientific journals are open access, which means you can find them and download them for free.

Reflections

There is much to discuss when it comes to the role of the internet in our lives and in society, including world politics. The history and, in particular, the sociological and political aspects of the internet vary between and also within countries. For example, internet connection has usually been better in cities than in distant rural areas. Moreover, telephone technology (e.g., 4G, 5G, mobile phone masts) and access to the internet are strongly connected. This reminds me that we should not forget that there are clients who do not have modern equipment or connection to the internet, which makes them outcasts in society as it is increasingly the case that internet access is needed for almost everything. One example here in Sweden is newspapers that are only available digitally and no longer delivered in the paper format. We may see the beginning of a counter movement with, for example, research on children and differences between reading on screen versus paper and people reducing their use of social media. In retrospect, the internet has not been with us for that long, and we may gradually find a balanced way to handle the technology and may even say no to some developments (with AI being one currently debated example).

5

How to set up a treatment platform

Without going into much detail, this chapter will cover the basic facts on how treatment platforms are set up. Recommendations will be given and also recommendations regarding security issues and legislation. Here I am relying on the work by the system programmer and developer George Vlaescu in my research group, and more detailed descriptions are available for the interested reader (Vlaescu et al., 2016, 2024). Interestingly, the development of ICBT was much helped by young psychologists who had a dual competence in web programming and CBT (Andersson, 2018). There are now numerous different systems/platforms, with some being more widely used and implemented (for example SilverCloud, Minddistrict, Stöd och Behandling (SOB) and the MindSpot Clinic system) and some mostly being used in research studies (like our Iterapi system). Moreover, online psychological services in the form of video therapy and added features are very common and took off even more during the pandemic years. I will mainly describe our own system Iterapi, but there are, as mentioned, many other systems and also some that have existed but now are gone.

Basically, treatment platforms are content management systems that often resemble online education resources used across the world at many universities and educational settings. Web-based platforms are used for presenting treatment contents using text, images, tables, films, audio files, game-like solutions, text and video chats, etc. It is crucial that the systems integrate different functions to generate a unified experience for the user. As described by Vlaescu et al. (2024), when presenting the Iterapi system, this includes a) content

DOI: 10.4324/9781003453444-6

management of treatment materials and public pages; b) user management by administrators and therapists, but also clients when they make choices in terms of treatment planning; c) planning of the treatment including when questionnaires should be completed and treatment modules be delivered, and also a calendar with notifications; and d) detailed configuration elements when it comes to layout, languages, time zones and formats, for example, responsive formats that are adapted based on device used, allowed operations. Procedures for data collection, handling and exporting are included. An example of a module selection screen is presented in Figure 5.1.

Established and well-developed treatment platforms can be used for other purposes than only treatment. I will discuss assessment

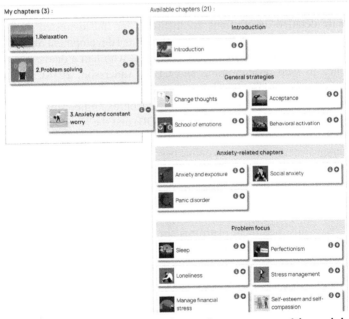

Figure 5.1 Screenshot from a depression program with module selection

procedures in the next chapter, but it should be mentioned that treatment platforms can also be used for educational purposes, for example, training courses for CBT clinicians (e.g., Atzor et al., 2024) and also for experimental studies (including mini- or single-session interventions like a study on New Year's resolutions). Further, platforms can be used for CBT supervision (as video conversation tools can be embedded) but also for filing notes in clinical services.

Platforms usually host several programs simultaneously on the platform, which saves both time and resources. Treatment programs and also specific research studies usually have their own home pages and are accessed via their own URL addresses. While previous material can be used including standard templates, programs tend to have adapted layouts, implemented from a number of templates in terms of colours, logos and page sections. I will return to the topic of adapting interventions for different target populations, but it is clearly the case that an intervention aimed for older adults will not look the same as a similar intervention (for example, for depression) for adolescents. Data management programs have their own database, allowing for a clear separation of data but also for security reasons.

While early platforms and web solutions used commercial services to host their programs (like web hotels), and some still do, it is sometimes demanded that service providers have their own servers and are in full control. I mentioned this as, for example, some universities in the United States are reluctant to accept that a server is located outside of the country, whereas most other places/universities do not consider this as a problem while still valuing security and control. Our Iterapi platform is hosted on designated servers located at Linköping University, Sweden, where we work. The hardware, operating system and infrastructure are provided by the IT department at our university, which ensures high-level stability and security (Vlaescu et al., 2016). The platform server uses Linux, with the operating system and packages automatically updated and monitored by system administrators. To further secure data management, daily backups of data from all programs are made with backup servers located in a different building at the university.

Security is crucial when delivering clinical services online and has been in focus since the early start of ICBT. Overall, access to user data need to be protected and strictly controlled including level of access to information. Data security is a moving target, with early treatment platforms usually having just one password to log in, but for a long time we have used multi-factor authentication with two separate sources. Both in Sweden and internationally, we have for long used one-time SMS codes as the second login step after providing the username and password. Increasingly, and also with the wide dissemination of smartphone technology, other ways to secure identity have emerged. This varies between countries, but electronic identification using third-party smartphone apps or services is increasingly used for internet banking or other public services, which lead clients to expect the same from online treatment services. In Sweden we have our own identification method called BankID, which is used by a majority of smartphone users and increasingly demanded to access online services needing identification (for example, when shopping on the internet). This saves time and resources for us and our clients but can also be a challenge as there is not an international solution, and it will be hard to implement all electronic ID systems on our platform. On a related note, it should be presented as an advantage that ICBT can be spread via translated and culturally adapted programs and that language is less of a barrier now with some program being presented in different languages so that the client can choose (see Chapter 13). I will return to this topic, but I expect that different language alternatives will be a requirement of most ICBT services in the future, not the least in order to work for global mental health.

Security also concerns data security overall. User information is stored and encrypted in the databases using specific algorithms, and it is also impossible to link the encrypted data to specific clients by only getting access to the database. All data communication is encrypted, and we, as most universities, have a security team at the university. This is also regulated on a national and even international level with, for example, the requirements imposed by General Data Protection Regulation (GDPR) and, in the United States, the Health Insurance Portability and Accountability Act (HIPAA).

Reflections

During my years working with ICBT, I have benefitted much from the skills and knowledge of my co-workers as I do not have any technical training or background myself. Some clinicians and students are talented and can create excellent web design features in terms of use of colours, pictures, logos, etc. Many CBT clinicians and researchers focus on what they see and can understand, which is not what is handled under the surface. For example, attractive web pages are often assumed to be important for treatment adherence, but I have always suspected that surface comes in as number two following functionality, with examples of studies having large dropout rates as participants failed to log in and then gave up. Both are important, of course, but user-friendliness/ease of navigation is crucial. The UX of a web solution is crucial, and sites need to be visually appealing, polished and professional. Added to that (under the surface but present with different log in procedures), security is key. Ten years back I believed that by now in 2024 biological identification would be present everywhere, but while face ID is used in smartphones, it may be that the technology is not fully accepted even if it is there. This leads me to another reflection I often return to, namely the importance of technology acceptance and standardization in order to avoid fatigue with too many changes. Some inventions are not used as much as we would have expected, and it is a historical fact that use of SMS was not expected when it became the most common use of mobile phones (in spite of bad ergonomics). Having said that, we now live with many technical facilities making life easier.

6

Internet-based assessment procedures

ICBT and CBT in general usually involve assessment procedures, and with the introduction of the internet in the 1990s, online questionnaires and other computerized assessment procedures were developed and subsequently tested in research. This is not only relevant for treatment but also for clinical practice and research in general. To give an example, experimental research on decision making and cognition is now dominated by large-scale online experiments, which have replaced laboratory tests to a large extent. Epidemiological surveys and outcome auditing of clinical services are now often conducted via online questionnaires. Further, given the almost-ubiquitous possession of smartphones, it is very common to complete questionnaires via the phone. In this chapter I will comment on the use of online questionnaires and other assessment procedures used in ICBT.

As a starting point and related to the previous chapter, platforms used for ICBT usually include assessment procedures as well. As clinical data by definition are sensitive, security issues apply (for example, encryption). There are several commercial solutions available, with Google Forms, SurveyMonkey and Qualtrics being three examples of questionnaire administration solutions. Most systems used are secure and have the legal work done, but things become a bit more complicated. When it comes to sensitive Electronic Health Records for the private practitioner, special programs are usually involved (for example, TheraNest, Charm and TherapyNotes). In Sweden Electronic Health Records are widely implemented in health care and have replaced paper notes, but it is still the case that this varies in the world.

DOI: 10.4324/9781003453444-7

There are things to consider when setting up a questionnaire booklet for research or clinical practice. Often, demographic information and other relevant background characteristics are included. It can also be useful to have initial screening questionnaires with automated summary score calculations in order to detect and sometimes refer clients or potential research participants to other services if needed. Completing questionnaires online can be fairly similar to the traditional paper-and-pencil format, but there are some advantages. For example, items in online questionnaires can be presented separately instead of having them all on the screen (as in the paper-and-pencil format). Online administration can also prevent skipping items, even if that option should be considered sometimes as clients may be irritated if they are "forced" to complete all items in order to proceed with an assessment procedure. Other advantages include adaptive testing, with follow-up questions only being asked following affirmative responses, screens that can be adapted for font size for persons with visual problems and progress bars to boost motivation to complete all measures. There are more advantages in terms of speed of scoring and providing feedback to the client, correction of spelling errors (in contrast to the old days when a spelling error in a printed questionnaire could be costly), and for clinical services it can be important to monitor deterioration and suicidal intent. For the clinician and researcher, online administration also saves time as there is no need to enter data manually to a computer file as data are exported directly from the systems. For live therapy sessions there are occasions when it can be good to administer a questionnaire on paper and then discuss the scoring with the client directly, but even that can be done via, for example, a tablet using a support system (Månsson, Ruiz, et al., 2013). An example of how a questionnaire may appear on the screen is presented in Figure 6.1.

There were some issues we considered when we began transferring paper-and-pencil questionnaires to the internet 20 years back which are still relevant. First, the technical aspects had to be handled. The next question was if online measures would work as well as traditional paper-and-pencil questionnaires. This led to several research studies comparing computer and paper administration

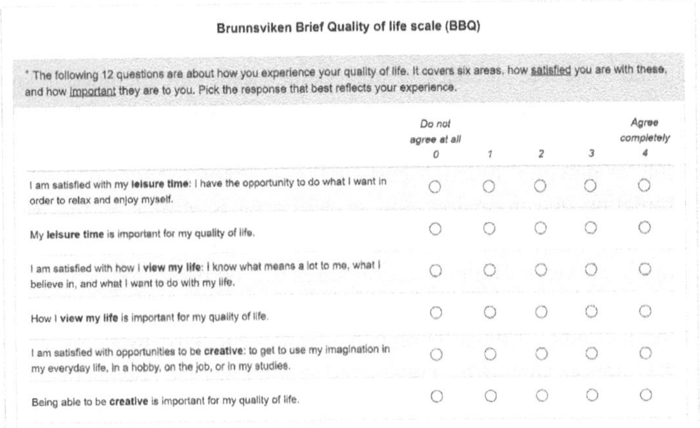

Brunnsviken Brief Quality of life scale (BBQ)

* The following 12 questions are about how you experience your quality of life. It covers six areas, how satisfied you are with these, and how important they are to you. Pick the response that best reflects your experience.

	Do not agree at all 0	*1*	*2*	*3*	*Agree completely* 4
I am satisfied with my **leisure time**: I have the opportunity to do what I want in order to relax and enjoy myself.	○	○	○	○	○
My **leisure time** is important for my quality of life.	○	○	○	○	○
I am satisfied with how I **view my life**: I know what means a lot to me, what I believe in, and what I want to do with my life.	○	○	○	○	○
How I **view my life** is important for my quality of life.	○	○	○	○	○
I am satisfied with opportunities to be **creative**: to get to use my imagination in my everyday life, in a hobby, on the job, or in my studies.	○	○	○	○	○
Being able to be **creative** is important for my quality of life.	○	○	○	○	○

Figure 6.1 Online questionnaire. Example: Brunnsviken Quality of Life Questionnaire

of questionnaires. The aim of this research was to establish that the transferred questionnaires had maintained psychometric properties, including internal consistency, factor structure and correlations with other constructs as their original versions. It is increasingly common that questionnaires are developed and tested ONLY in their online format, but in order to be able to compare results from the earlier days with paper-and-pencil norms, it is relevant to reflect upon the differences when interpreting test results.

Now in 2024 we have established and detailed guidelines for technology-based assessments issued by the *International Test Commission and Association of Test Publishers* (2022). Briefly, they give recommendations on test development and, for example, how the use of technology might affect assessment of the constructs of interest. This includes impact on measurement properties such as reliability and correlations with other constructs, but also non-psychometric features such as costs of technology versus expected benefits. When different administration formats are used, it can be important to secure that they measure the same thing as the original measure with comparable means and standard deviations and reliabilities, but as we now see much research on measures without any paper-and-pencil data, this is sometimes less relevant. However, from a clinical point of view, there can be situations when paper administration is called for, and then the question becomes relevant again when interpreting a measure that has been developed and validated for online use only. The test commission comments on the specific added value with computer administration such as additional instructions (for example, a video illustrating how the assessment will be done for the test takers), possibilities to reach test takers with poorer internet access and how technology can support test takers with disabilities and with different language backgrounds.

Questionnaires

There are several published research studies conducted by ICBT researchers on the administration of questionnaires over the internet. Many established clinical self-report measures have been used in ICBT research, and in a systematic review paper by van Ballegooijen et al. (2016), 62 online instruments could be included, reported in a total of 56 studies. Overall, adequate psychometric properties had been reported in the studies, and the authors found at least one online measure for each of the included mental health disorders and symptoms. Some measures have been more evaluated including different target groups and languages, and as I mentioned, much scale development research is now done online. Moreover, it is increasingly common to report basic measurement characteristics such as baseline means, standard deviations and internal consistency (Cronbach's alpha coefficient) in treatment trials and not as separate publications. This can be phrased as "in the present study Cronbach's alpha was .91 for the XYZ measure". This is good scientific practice even if it makes it a bit more difficult to find updated information on psychometric properties of measures used. Overall, since the publication of my previous book on ICBT 10 years back, online administration of self-report questionnaires used in ICBT and in CBT in general is now standard procedure. Research on daily administered measures, often described as ecological momentary assessment (EMA), has been much facilitated by use of online data collection by means of smartphones (Colombo et al., 2019), and this has also included sensors and other forms of data collection than self-report measures (Mohr et al., 2017). I will later on comment on interventions based on EMA, which is a clinically derived use of EMA technology.

Back in 2015 I commented that in many ways it could be argued that online measurements had not taken advantage of the computer media enough (Andersson, 2015). This may change now with the increased use of AI, and one interesting development could be to collect idiosyncratic language data and use AI-informed language models to analyse the results (Kjell et al., 2019). This could be a revival of individualized measures that were often used in the early days of CBT (in particular, behaviour therapy) but suffered from poor measurement characteristics.

Diagnostic procedures

While self-report questionnaires work well over the internet and even have advantages over paper-and-pencil measures, complete diagnostic procedures cannot be delivered via the internet without any clinician interaction. This has been known for a long time and is based on the observation that procedures which rely on self-report do not correspond sufficiently well with the results of an interview with a trained clinician (Martin-Key et al., 2022). Telephone or video administration of structured psychiatric interviews do a better job and will, in my experience, complement the results from self-report questionnaires. While video (now often using systems like Zoom and Microsoft Teams) may provide added information, it is not clear from research that there are major benefits compared to voice-only telephone interviews (Chen et al., 2022). It is possible that research will be done using chatbots mimicking a live clinician, but again that needs to be first tested in comparative research, and at the end of the day it will also be a question of preference. Moreover, there can be issues related to patient security, insurance and also monetary reasons (in order to be able to charge for services) to see clients at least once in a "real-time" video or telephone meeting. I will return to assessment in Chapter 15 on the treatment process in ICBT.

Performance measures including cognitive tests

Early on researchers considered the possibility of administering computerized cognitive tests including neuropsychological measures online, which often can be a feasible alternative to face-to-face assessments (Binoy et al., 2023). In research, online tests of selective information processing lead to many experimental studies on measures like the Stroop Task, the Implicit Association Test and the Visual Dot Probe Task, just to give just three examples. Increasingly, the reliability of such tests have been in focus, and it has been recommended that researchers in this field report psychometric properties of their tests. Research on the role of cognition in psychopathology is an important part of CBT and has therefore also influenced ICBT. Technological advancements have a great potential in this research, for example, using augmented reality to test selective attention in anxiety, even if most research focus on treatment (Carlson, 2023). On a related note, there have been several studies on bias modification paradigms, which I will return to in the next chapter.

Reflections

Internet-based assessment procedures are abundant, and, as with many things on the internet, users (including both clinicians and clients) tend to go for the free versions; and there is an inherent difficulty for test publishers to protect their publishing rights and also a tendency for us clinicians and researchers to go for the free versions, for example, the PHQ-9. It is easy to imagine a different world in which information was less free and open access publishing of research (in which, for example, new questionnaires are described and author contact provided to facilitate requests for permission to use the test, etc.) did not exist. On the other hand, the preference for low or no costs has potentially slowed down the dissemination of other test procedures like cognitive testing, and *International Test Commission and Association of Test Publishers* has an important role here to provide recommendations and advice. As we now most likely face a new era of computer use with AI, it will be increasingly important to agree on the standards. For example, translation and cultural adaption of tests (see more on this in Chapter 13) will be done in seconds with the use of programs like Chat GPT and Google's Gemini (and most likely other programs when you read this text).

7

Use of smartphone apps, wearables, gamification, virtual reality and cognitive bias modification

In this chapter I will cover a large topic with a focus on what is relevant for ICBT, even if there are numerous smartphone applications, including wearables, that can be used as part of a CBT treatment like, for example, a sports app (e.g., Runkeeper and Nike's Training Club) to track physical activity and sleep apps to measure sleep (like SleepScore), etc. In other words, CBT clinicians may recommend apps in their clinical everyday practice, but there is very limited research on how common this is. In fact, it is often the case that we do not know how clinicians use information from such technology, and it is the same when it comes to recommending YouTube videos, TV programs, books, etc. As I mentioned earlier, previous studies show that almost nine out of 10 recommend self-help material in their clinical CBT practice, and self-help material is often regarded as part of CBT (Bohman et al., 2017; Keeley et al., 2002).

Smartphone apps

When it comes to smartphone apps, much research has been devoted to the effects of using them (Zale et al., 2021). The literature is a bit difficult to evaluate as different technologies often are mixed in studies, and that blended treatments (for example, when a research participant meet the therapist on a few occasions to get support and instructions on how to use the app) often are included when the evidence is evaluated. Moreover, as described

DOI: 10.4324/9781003453444-8

in Chapter 5, ICBT platforms should preferably be responsive, meaning that they adapt the presentation/screen based on the device used. This means that it is less crucial to download and install an app on your phone, with the exception of when there is a need for having the app installed for collecting certain kinds of data (for example, activity monitoring without self-report). Clients tend to prefer to be able to choose a device, and in our recent research studies, many users of our Iterapi system often log in with their smartphone but may prefer to sit in front of a tablet or computer screen at home as it is easier to complete measures and read texts that way. On the other hand, there are over 10,000 mental health apps commercially available that are often informed by CBT but not full CBT treatment programs and even more rarely tested in controlled outcome research. In a consensus statement (Torous et al., 2019), we gave many recommendations regarding the use of mental health apps. Among these were recommendations regarding data management and storing, including security. We also recommended that new apps undergo controlled clinical trials, and also called for a consistent terminology in order to evaluate both benefits and risks of using an app. This is one major concern I have as the difference between two apps for the same clinical condition can be vast and can range between a minimal intervention to a library of many techniques and resources in the app. In the statement, we also called for more use of user-centred/user experience (UX) design methods and also standards for best practice in user design research for mental health apps. This is also relevant for ICBT in general, as there is no clear consensus regarding UX research in the field of internet interventions. Another and perhaps more complicated issue is to embed mental health apps into existing health care systems in a secure manner. Here in Sweden we have that for our tax-funded health care system (called 1177), but that is not the same as having mental health apps easily available and linked to the system as these apps tend to be developed by companies. Indeed the ICBT system most frequently used in Swedish health care (I will return to that later) called "Stöd och behandling" is not an app.

But what about the effects of CBT delivered via smartphones? Here we have the same distinction between guided and unguided interventions as in the field of ICBT in general. Publicly available mental health apps without any interaction with a clinician can be useful but cannot be regarded as evidence-based to the same extent as guided treatments. When guidance is provided, including proper diagnostic interviews, smartphone-delivered interventions have been found to work well in controlled studies on, for example, depression (Moshe et al., 2021; Ly et al., 2014). An example of a smartphone presentation of an ICBT program in Lithuanian is presented in Figure 7.1.

Wearables and sensors

Sometimes connected to smartphones are wearables and different kind of sensors, which can be defined as any device that detects and measures a physical property (Mohr et al., 2017). Sensors of physical properties, such as heart rate and skin conductance, have been much researched in the field of psychophysiology, with most studies done in labs. When measuring such variables using smartphones, additional devices might be needed such as wearable devices (for example, a belt over the chest to measure heart rate), but increasingly sensors are embedded in the phone or wristwatch. In a review of different sensors, Mohr et al. (2017) gave several examples of how sensors are used for measuring, for example, sleep activity, individual moments, smartphone use (like time spent on social media), speech patterns and postural balance. Many readers will recognize this from what they have in their phones. The technology moves fast, and increasingly monitoring applications of devices like a pacemaker or a hearing aid are developed and used. It is a bit uncertain what sensor data (not including self-reported mood) add to the description of mood states, and how such data can inform CBT, but I would welcome more research on use of sensors in studies of behavioural activation in depression (which was part of a project called the ICT4Depression I worked with) and measures

Kalbu viešai

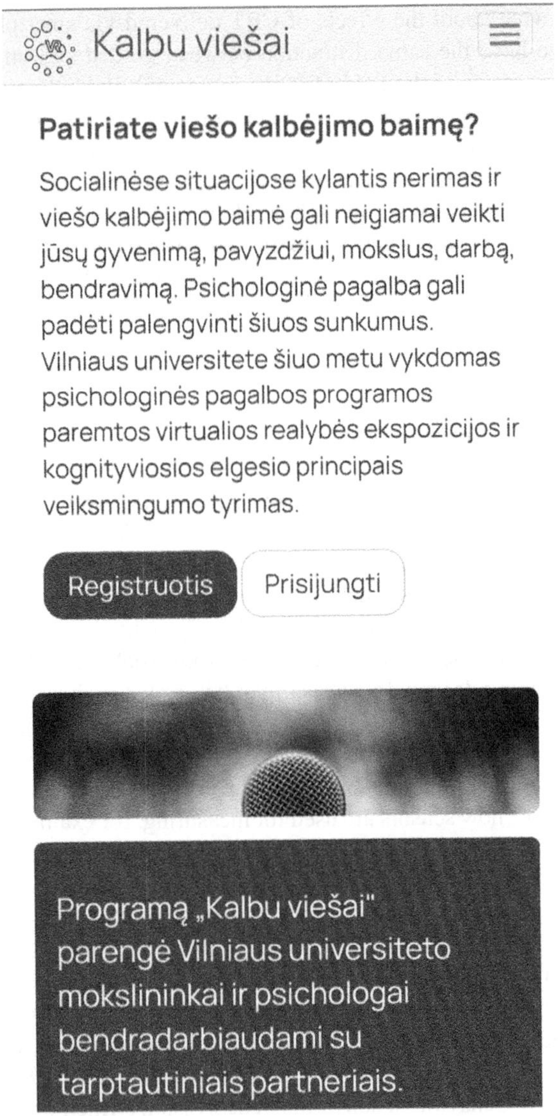

Patiriate viešo kalbėjimo baimę?

Socialinėse situacijose kylantis nerimas ir viešo kalbėjimo baimė gali neigiamai veikti jūsų gyvenimą, pavyzdžiui, mokslus, darbą, bendravimą. Psichologinė pagalba gali padėti palengvinti šiuos sunkumus. Vilniaus universitete šiuo metu vykdomas psichologinės pagalbos programos paremtos virtualios realybės ekspozicijos ir kognityviosios elgesio principais veiksmingumo tyrimas.

Registruotis   Prisijungti

Programą „Kalbu viešai" parengė Vilniaus universiteto mokslininkai ir psichologai bendradarbiaudami su tarptautiniais partneriais.

Figure 7.1 Mobile phone presentation view in Lithuanian

34

of blood pressure and heart rate in studies on relaxation and mind-fulness, for which there is some ongoing work. Sensors are also highly relevant in medicine, for example, in studies on balance in the elderly.

Serious games and gamification

ICBT can be perceived as rather stiff and boring by younger persons as it resembles school education, and therefore researchers and clinicians have, for a long time, worked on gamification of CBT techniques (adding gaming elements), and also on serious games (in which CBT techniques are presented in a game). This is not only relevant for children and younger persons, even if it might be more important for the younger clients. One early example of a computerized CBT game was the program SPARX for adolescents with symptoms of depression, which resembled the computer program Sims (Merry et al., 2012). Fleming et al. (2016) provided three reasons to consider serious games: extending reach of internet treatments for persons who would not use them otherwise; improving engagement; and finally delivering important change processes via games. I would like to add that gamification often has been included in different ICBT treatment programs on, for example, anxiety in children 8–12 years old (Vigerland, Ljótsson, et al., 2016). One aspect that I believe has slowed down the development and use of serious games in CBT is the cost of programming and the difficulties producing CBT-oriented games that do not appear obsolete too quickly. Potentially, medico-legal aspects and the fact the gamification more easily can be embedded in ICBT programs than to develop separate serious games may also have slowed down the research and dissemination, even if there are several exciting projects and studies. For example, there are many possibilities and different forms of games such as Exergames that are sport- or movement-based, virtual reality games (more on this soon), entertainment computer games (for example, use of the game *Tetris* in research on trauma), biofeedback games and finally cognitive training games (Fleming et al., 2016). To the best of my knowledge, there is yet limited research, and in particular on the use of online games as part of a CBT treatment with existing games and how well a serious game works compared to other treatments such as ICBT in the usual format. There is also limited research and even descriptions of how gamification procedures have been incorporated in ICBT and how it is perceived.

Virtual reality

Virtual reality (VR) should be mentioned, as it can be used along-side ICBT programs and delivered via the internet (Carlson, 2023). I will be brief here as this is a large field that has existed for many years, and it has only more recently been possible to transfer from the lab to the public (Lindner et al., 2017). Many readers may have tested a virtual reality application which is commonly described as computer-generated environments with visual presentations, sounds and sometimes even physical (haptic) stimulations that make the situation appear to be real or life-like as the user is immersed in the VR surrounding. Another related technique is augmented or mixed reality in which real-world and computer-generated content are combined (for example, by wearing glasses that present spiders in the room in exposure therapy). There is a large number of studies on topics like specific phobias, social anxiety disorder, substance use disorders (SUD) and post-traumatic stress disorder (PTSD) suggesting that VR works. In particular, in exposure therapies for animal phobias and heights, VR serves as a feasible alternative to exposure to real objects, with some studies suggesting that it works almost as well as in-vivo exposure (Miloff et al., 2019). As covering VR and augmented reality applications in full would require a full book, I will just conclude that the technology exists and that it is less costly now with the use of smartphones than before when VR required a visit to a lab or clinic. But I am also wondering why CBT clinicians do not use VR more often, and, as acknowledged in the field, there are, for some clients, negative reactions and even nausea (cyber sickness) or discomfort associated with use of VR. The role of the therapist in VR has also been acknowledged and also the use of VR as part of a CBT or ICBT treatment (Ma et al., 2021).

Cognitive bias modification

Again with the caveat that I need to be brief (as with VR given that it is a large field on its own), cognitive bias modification (CBM) techniques have been developed and tested over the internet and also combined with ICBT. There are several different cognitive processes that CBM can target, but an overall definition of CBM is the use of repeated practice on cognitive tasks that are associated with vulnerability for anxiety, depression and other clinically relevant problems (Hertel & Mathews, 2011). It should be mentioned that CBM has stirred up some debate within CBT with conflicting results and also diverging interpretations of studies and their results. CBM can be divided into programs that target: a) *attention bias modification*, with, for example, selective attention in social anxiety disorder being one example; b) *interpretation bias modification*, with programs focusing on, for example, intrusive images in PTSD and negative thinking in major depression; c) *memory bias modification/practice*, with, for example, generating specific concrete memories rather than overgeneral non-specific memories in depression; and d) *approach-avoidance training*, with programs involving training of visual stimuli related to, for example, alcohol in substance use disorders or anger-provoking faces for persons with anger management problems. This may sound odd, but it involves selectively inducing avoidance of one type of stimulus and/or approach of another. There are several meta-analysis on the effects of CBM. It is fair to conclude that CBM can work (Jones & Sharpe, 2017) but that there is still not sufficient evidence to conclude that CBM works as well as regular face-to-face CBT or even guided ICBT. However, combinations of formats, with, for example, CBM techniques being incorporated in ICBT programs, may be used given that the procedures work and are accepted by clients.

Reflections

In this chapter I covered several different technologies that are used to deliver CBT content and of relevance for ICBT. While smartphone applications are by far the most commonly used technique among the ones reviewed, gamification/serious games and virtual reality applications are the focus of some development/research and can be integrated with ICBT. In my impression CBM has more recently attained somewhat less research interest. Another impression from that research is that it did not really fulfil the expectations, with some null findings and inconsistent research. This might change, and I do believe that CBM approaches lend themselves to be combined with ICBT, but also gamification and virtual reality. Three important processes should be considered when using technological solutions in CBT. First and foremost, user experience and feasibility is key. If, for example, a technique for CBM is perceived as boring and not intuitive, it may not work because of poor adherence. If virtual reality is experienced by too many as unpleasant, it will also suffer from the same problem. Second, and perhaps obvious, the change process targeted by the technique must be relevant and important. If, for example, a client does not behave in a way consistent with theory in terms of avoiding, for example, eye contact in social anxiety disorder, CBM might not work as well. This is not unique for CBM but concerns psychotherapy in general. Third, technology changes sometimes rapidly, which calls for resources for updating and maintaining technology. This is an aspect that has had major negative impact on smartphone apps as companies go out of business and services are not maintained. It also concerns how much we need programmers, and while that is of course of importance in ICBT overall, it is somewhat less difficult in ICBT as maintaining and updating a website in terms of content often can be done with less-skilled staff, whereas updating a VR application still requires other programming skills. It may be that the rapid AI development will have implications for those aspect as well if we can ask the computer to implement changes in our programs.

8

Video therapy

Video consultations have existed for a long time and have been framed within the larger field of telemedicine/telehealth. CBT clinicians have, for a long time, had contact with their clients and even provided full CBT over the telephone, but as video conferencing became more available with the internet, video became another option (albeit sometimes held back by security regulations). Video conferencing as a way to provide CBT has oddly not been much focused in research, and the same goes for telephone-delivered CBT. There is research done, but not that much as on ICBT (Chen et al., 2022). Here I will focus on the use of real-time video chats/video-delivered CBT, as it is highly relevant for the practice of ICBT. During the pandemic years we saw a dramatic increase in the use and acceptance of video therapy delivered online. In fact, it is probably more likely now that clients expect video therapy when hearing about ICBT (which is usually based on self-help material and does not involve real-time video therapy sessions). It is also now more common following the pandemic that clients have experience of video consultations for mental health problems, but also for health problems in general. I will comment on a few aspects related to the use of online video conferencing methods and also comment on telephone consultation and therapy.

First, use of video for diagnostic interviews can serve as an alternative to face-to-face consultations in the field of mental health, and it can be argued that the visual information provided helps, even if telephone administration of structured interviews has been found to be useful as well and often more easy to access. At least that

DOI: 10.4324/9781003453444-9

was the case before, but now when many clients have smartphones, it is rather preferences that influence the choice to only use telephone without video. The main point here is the fact that diagnostic procedures using validated questionnaires often need to be complemented with interviews (see Chapter 6) and may also serve to motivate clients to continue with ICBT.

Second, studies have been done on both telephone-only and on video-delivered CBT, with overall evidence suggesting that the formats can work and potentially be as effective as face-to-face CBT even if there are fairly few direct comparisons (Chen et al., 2022). To add complexity to our understanding of the literature, there are also studies and treatment programs in which video, telephone, ICBT (mainly guided self-help) and face-to-face consultations are blended, which I view as a natural consequence of having more than one way to work and stay in contact with our clients. For example, clinicians sometimes continue CBT treatments with video meetings (following initial face-to-face contact) if, for example, the client (or therapist) move or is away for travel. As with many things in the real and changing world, I do not know how common this is, but at least it is likely to be more common and accepted now following the pandemic years. But as clinical services need to be funded, it is increasingly questioned if reimbursement for a video consultation should equal a face-to-face meeting. In Sweden, video-delivered CBT with sessions being shortened has also been questioned as short sessions do not necessarily correspond to what has been tested in research. Having said that, there are controlled studies and evidence suggesting that both phone- and video-delivered CBT can be effective for conditions like anxiety/depression, PTSD, SUD, eating disorders and obsessive-compulsive disorder (OCD), just to give a few examples (Chen et al., 2022). But as both telephone and video CBT have been less researched compared to ICBT, there are still uncertainties regarding long-term effects and cost-effectiveness, and also client preferences and satisfaction. There are some studies on therapeutic alliance in video CBT (and in telephone CBT), and overall client perception of their therapist does not seem to suffer much from the distance format (Schoenenberg & Martin, 2024). I believe that mixed research methods using both quantitative and qualitative methods can inform us as clinicians and researchers about the pros and cons of video/telephone delivery, and it is important to note that even if two formats work as well in terms of reducing symptoms, they may work via different change mechanisms and may be viewed differently by clients.

My third comment relates to practical issues. In our internet treatment platform *Iterapi*, video conversations are available in the platform, which makes a separate video application not needed (see Chapter 5). But for many readers, again referring to Chapter 5, it can be a question of costs, and it can be tempting to use services like Zoom and Microsoft Teams, just to give two examples. In spite of technical issues, it is also a question of preferences, and while the difference between ICBT (guided self-help) and face-to-face CBT cannot be missed and is clear in terms of what can be expected (for example, having access 24/7 to the program and rapid response when sending questions to therapists in ICBT versus scheduled video meetings and no contact in between sessions), it is less clear what to expect in real-time video CBT versus face-to-face CBT. In any case, clinicians delivering ICBT can consider using video sessions as a complement and even as part of their treatment. Clinicians who now continue to use video as a tool should consider ICBT as a complement and even self-help books. Researchers should also evaluate such blending of services.

Reflections

When returning to this topic, it is fairly clear that use of video as a CBT delivery format is in need of more research. With ICBT, we know fairly well from large effectiveness/pragmatic studies how well the treatment works in regular clinical practice. This is less well known for telephone and video conversations. As I return to many times in this book, we may see increased use of AI chatbots and video conversations with non-human counterparts. It may even develop to the extent that it will be hard to detect if it is a live therapist or a virtual one. When it comes to regular telephone conversations with a therapist, they can already now be assisted or even replaced with AI-generated material.

9

Specific assumptions and theories

The content and treatment procedures in ICBT are mostly based on existing CBT theories, and there is not much published on specific theories for ICBT or internet interventions overall. Common psychological theories on behaviour and cognitive change are relevant to consider and have indeed been used. One example is the *Theory of Planned Behaviour*, which was outlined first by Ajzen (1991) and says that three core components: attitudes, subjective norms and perceived behavioural control, together shape an individual's behavioural intentions. This theory is often referred to when developing treatments and has been associated with improved outcomes in internet interventions (Webb et al., 2010). Another well-known theory from psychology is *the self-efficacy theory* by Bandura (1977), which is related to several other theoretical perspectives such as social-cognitive, learning and attribution theories, just to give three examples. While perhaps self-evident and well known by many readers, the concept of self-efficacy relates to an individual's belief in his/her capacity to act in the ways necessary to reach desired goals. In lay terms, concepts like self-esteem and self-confidence, but also outcome expectancies, are relevant. The self-efficacy concept has been much used in research, and in particular it is relevant for health care and health behaviours. In ICBT research, self-efficacy is sometimes measured generating both meaningful correlations (including mediation and prediction of dropout) but also direct effects (Johansson et al., 2022; Schønning & Nordgreen, 2021). However, with a few exceptions, my impression is that the established and old concept of self-efficacy has not been

DOI: 10.4324/9781003453444-10

in much focus for theory development (apart from being included as a measure in many studies), in spite of the fact that self-help treatments, almost by definition, involve self-efficacy.

The few theories relevant for ICBT specifically have focused on how the delivery format makes a difference, rather than the change mechanisms associated with certain therapeutic techniques. It could be argued that a CBT technique like exposure works via the same mechanisms regardless of whether the rationale and instructions for practice in real life (e.g., homework) are presented by a therapist in a therapy room, or via the internet in the form of text, including perhaps a video. But even if the delivery format might not matter, it is still very different and may also involve practice using the treatment program (for example, giving a speech in front of a virtual audience in ICBT for social anxiety). Therefore, we need good ideas and a theoretical understanding of what occurs in ICBT, and in particular what promotes adherence and motivation. We also need theoretical understanding to prevent treatment failure or just not engaging in the treatment. Here I will mention some perspectives/theories that have been proposed and also a review paper summarizing several theoretical approaches. I will then move on and comment on my own assumptions and experiences from working in the field for 25 years.

Ritterband et al. (2009) proposed a behavioural change model specific for internet interventions. Briefly, the model describes nine steps that are regarded as influential, with each one not necessarily following the other. The model highlights the importance of the *user*, the influence of *environmental factors*, the effect of *website use* and *consequent adherence* and also the influence of *support* and *website characteristics*. It was suggested in the paper that website use leads to *behaviour change* and *symptom improvement* through various *mechanisms of change*, with improvements being sustained via *treatment maintenance*. Readers may note that in this model the practice of CBT techniques is not put forward, but rather how actual computer use makes a difference. As mentioned earlier, it is one thing to give instructions via the internet on how to do exercises in vivo versus doing exposure via the computer (like my example of giving a speech in front of a virtual audience in social anxiety disorder treatment).

A later model specific for how support influences the effects of internet treatments was proposed by Mohr et al. (2011). This model, called "supportive accountability", was informed by research on organizational psychology, motivation theory and computer-mediated communication. The model suggests that the function of human support in internet interventions is to increase adherence as the therapist/coach is viewed as trustworthy, benevolent and having expertise. Research on the role of therapeutic alliance in ICBT is in line with this reasoning (more on the alliance is covered in Chapter 14). Some predictions were made that are plausible and to some extent supported in research. For example, that clients with intrinsic motivation for change will be in less need for support. What may complicate this idea is that the program in itself may be viewed as supportive and that the voice of the therapist can be present in the self-help material. On the other hand, studies on self-guided ICBT (with no contact during the treatment phase except for automated reminders) suggests that a proportion of clients do equally well without support as when guidance/human support is provided. Mohr et al. further argued that the effect of accountability is likely to be moderated by how motivated the client is, but also the media used for communication. I suspect that having interactions with the therapist in an asynchronous manner is different than real-time interaction, and further that it makes a difference if the client can return to the communication thread or not.

A third perspective and theoretical account was presented by Yardley et al. (2015), who promoted a "person-based" approach to help our understanding of how to make effective interventions. This model is perhaps more aimed for developers of treatment programs and highlights the importance of user experiences in order to enhance the theory and evidence-based procedures used to achieve intended changes following treatment. The approach involves a development process using qualitative research and views of different stakeholders, not only at the start but at each step of development. The second part of the person-based approach is to derive principles that can be used to inform further development. In my understanding, the "person-based" makes much sense, even if I also believe in a "Bayesian" principle, with lessons learned from earlier treatment development and testing informing the next project. The most important principle I use in my own research is to learn from experience and data. In other words, once we have the data it will be possible to get tentative answers that will inform the next program and/or study. An iterative process leaving room for innovation as well as recycling material and procedures is, in my experience, often feasible. Investigating both client and clinician experience of working with a treatment program can be much informative, not only to find aspects that need to be changed or updated but also for knowing what to retain, as change is not always for good.

Ryan et al. (2018) did a scoping review on what drives treatment adherence and engagement in internet interventions and covered several theoretical perspectives. These were the Internet Intervention Model, Persuasive Systems Design, the "PERMA" framework, the Support Accountability Model, the Model of User Engagement, the Technology Acceptance Model, the Unified Theory of Acceptance and Use of IT and the Conceptual Model of User Engagement. Briefly, the Internet Intervention Model was the one proposed by Ritterband et al. (2009), and the Support Accountability Model the one described by Mohr et al. (2011). The Persuasive Systems Design model represents a commonly discussed theme in internet intervention research, namely the importance and use of persuasive technology. Again, here it can be summarized as a perspective that focus on the role of technology for promoting change and recommendation on program design such as being easily available and open, incremental, unobtrusive, useful and easy to use, capable to foster user commitment and cognitive consistency and that persuasion (or, in other words, influence) may occur directly or indirectly (Oinas-Kukkonen & Harjumaa, 2009). The 'PERMA' framework is related to system design as well and suggests five components to be considered when designing internet interventions and increasing adherence (Ludden et al., 2015). These are the promotion of positive emotion, engagement, relationships, meaning and accomplishment (e.g., PERMA). Moreover, the importance of personalization, control and reduction of ambient information (referring to the flow of information on the internet and in phones) and use of metaphors were highlighted in the PERMA paper. The last three theories/models described by Ryan et al. (2018) are from the fields of information systems design, business and computing, and I will not comment on these here. There are by now numerous perspectives and also "moving targets" when it comes to use of technology, and it is beyond the scope here to cover the whole field. It is, however, very clear that, for example, technology acceptance makes a great difference as we have seen earlier when disseminating ICBT to places in the world where use of the internet in health care is not that spread or viewed with suspicion. More on this when we come to cultural adaption.

Reflections

ICBT and internet interventions in general have been the focus of much research. Given this large literature, numerous theoretical perspectives have been involved in intervention research, with a focus on the theories behind the treatment programs (for example, acceptance theory in ICBT studies on treatments based on ACT). Further, at least in my own research, we have prioritized developing new treatments and conducting studies, perhaps at the expense of generating new clinical theories and testing those, as has been done in clinical CBT research (Clark, 2004). On the other hand, it is perhaps more a question of what has been spelled out rather than a lack of theory. For example, after 10 years of ICBT research, we wrote a paper on "What makes internet therapy work" (Andersson, Carlbring, et al., 2009), in which we proposed that four components are relevant to make the treatment work: a) a proper diagnosis/assessment before the treatment starts, b) a comprehensive treatment, c) that the treatment is user-friendly and not overly technically advanced and d) support and a clear deadline are provided for the duration of the treatment. My impression is that this still applies and that these "lessons learned" could be framed in more theoretical terms such as reinforcement (learning theory), and indeed the self-efficacy theory, as well as the more specific theories on internet treatments such as supported accountability. Added to those, I also believe in the concept of the "therapeutic window", which is derived from pharmaceutical research (actually more related to medication dosage but can also apply to patient/ treatment matching). Basically, this means that a client may be either in the middle of the window in which the treatment fits well with the needs and motivation of the client. On the left side of the window are clients who have just minor problems and for which a full ICBT treatment would not be suitable. Here is where much prevention research resides, with the common problem that persons with a minor or even no problem tend to be less motivated to do a preventive treatment. On the right hand of the window, we have the very severe clients for which guided self-help is not suitable – at least not now. While psychiatric diagnoses may help us to some extent in locating where the client is on this continuum, I argue that this is not sufficient and that we also need to consider adapting our intervention to help the client get into the therapeutic window and also consider combined treatments when the client needs more treatment. The concept of the therapeutic window can also be used within a treatment to describe the 'sweet spot' between engagement and disengagement or, in ICBT, if a treatment module is feasible or not. The concept of the therapeutic window has been applied in many settings, including trauma and neurological rehabilitation, and makes much clinical sense.

10

ICBT as education

With its origin in bibliotherapy, ICBT benefits from previous bib-liotherapy research, and one aspect that is often ignored in CBT is the role of knowledge acquisition. Indeed, much of CBT consists of education, confidence in the knowledge and then courage to act in line with the new ideas and acquired knowledge obtained in therapy (including direct application in session or later as home-work). This is also commonly described as the *treatment rationale*, and most CBT clinicians would agree that presenting a rationale for a treatment procedure like exposure is key and that the client must understand the rationale in order to proceed with the technique. For example, if the client does not grasp the point with scheduled worry time in the treatment of generalized anxiety disorder, it will become very strange for the client if the therapist tells you to worry when that is what you have problems with. Oddly, with the exception of ICBT research in Israel, there is almost no research on what could be called "insight", which is one dimension of what I refer to here as knowledge.

Scogin et al. (1998) developed and tested a "cognitive biblio-therapy test" in order to be able to measure what clients knew before bibliotherapy and learned after completed treatment. This inspired us to develop a test in a trial on social anxiety disorder (Andersson, Carlbring, et al., 2012), with a pre-runner being an unpublished test and study on generalized anxiety disorder. The idea was further informed by work on psychoeducation, mental health literacy and the fact that clients and also clinicians may fail to remember what has been said during a face-to-face therapy session (or presented

DOI: 10.4324/9781003453444-11

in a self-help program). Likewise, therapists can fail to remember the specific details of their clients in session (for example, that the patient had informed the therapist that she was going to her daughter's wedding the upcoming weekend). Psychologist Matilda Berg did her PhD thesis in 2021 on the topic of knowledge with the title "Just know it: The role of explicit knowledge in internet-based cognitive behaviour therapy for adolescents". The thesis is a comprehensive summary of what is known about CBT and knowledge. Another important contribution to this topic is the work by Harvey et al. (2014), who focused on how memory and learning can be enhanced by considered pedagogy and what is known about education. The basic idea promoted by our research group is that ICBT can be conceptualized as a form of online patient education, and, as described in Chapter 5, the platforms used for ICBT tend to resemble learning platforms used in, for example, university education.

From a more practical point of view, client knowledge about problems and treatment procedures might not sound so difficult to define, but knowledge is in itself something that has a very long history for us humans and has been commented on in numerous texts. I will just be brief here, but a few categories of knowledge should be mentioned (Brewin, 1996). First we have *declarative and explicit knowledge*, which concerns consciously available information of episodic and semantic nature. This is the form of knowledge that more easily can be tested in knowledge tests. Second, we have *implicit knowledge* (also referred to as non-declarative), which involves perceptual and procedural memories not necessarily involving our conscious awareness such as motor skills, habits and when a behaviour becomes automatized. This could, in the context of ICBT, be measured by sensors in the smartphone measuring physical movements in behavioural activation treatment for depression, but overall it is more difficult to measure this form of learning even if it, from a theoretical point of view, could be an important change process in CBT (when, for example, social interaction becomes more of a habit without much reflection and worry for a former social anxiety disorder client). In CBT, and in particular cognitive therapy, constructs that are a form of knowledge have been promoted and used to inform treatment such as *meta-cognitive knowledge* (Wells, 2009) and *self-reflective knowledge* (Bennett-Levy et al., 2015). Basically this concerns what you recognize and know about your own thinking and learning, which are highly relevant in CBT overall.

Knowledge can also be categorized as being on different levels. The education researcher Hattie (2009) suggested three levels of knowledge: a) surface knowledge, b) deeper understanding and thinking ability and c) constructive knowledge. For ICBT it could be argued that all levels are important but that certain techniques require a deeper understanding and thinking ability. It can also be important to develop constructive knowledge to be able to draw new conclusions about life. There are other ways to divide knowledge with levels reflecting factual knowledge, conceptual knowledge, procedural knowledge and meta-cognitive knowledge (Berg, 2021). Again, all four of these are relevant for ICBT. When we discuss knowledge it is also relevant to consider how knowledge relates to learning. Learning can also be categorized in levels and categories such as verbal learning versus motor learning. In lay terms, use of these terms are not consistent, but it is usually held that learning is the process that leads to changes in levels of knowledge. Also it is often held that learning has occurred when the knowledge can be retrieved and applied in various situations. Much can be discussed on this topic on, for example, what happens following exposure and if something can be unlearnt versus just forgotten at this very moment.

Measurement of explicit knowledge

Over the years we have developed knowledge tests in association with controlled trials for different conditions and problems. I give example items in Table 10.1 here from a study we did on eating disorders (Strandskov et al., 2017) and one on depression (Andersson et al., 2023).

Table 10.1 Example items from knowledge test used in ICBT

Examples of eating disorders items

1. What is the most important thing to consider in CBT for eating disorders?
- a. To attend early warning signals for risk behaviours and use the tools acquired in treatment to handle those situations.
- b. To avoid difficult situations where risk behaviours can be elicited as it is easy to fall back to old bad eating habits.
- c. To avoid negative thoughts linked to eating disorders.

Rate how certain you are with your answer?
- 1. I am guessing
- 2. I am rather sure
- 3. I am almost certain
- 4. I am certain

2. Why is it important to be able to accept negative emotions?
- a. To get in touch with your feelings in order to be able to handle them.
- b. To make it easier to get rid of negative thoughts and get at new perspective.
- c. To make the positive thoughts more clear in order to be able to focus on them.

Rate how certain you are with your answer?
- 1. I am guessing
- 2. I am rather sure
- 3. I am almost certain
- 4. I am certain

Examples of depression items

1. According to CBT what is the best way to handle anxiety in the long run?
- a. To avoid anxiety provoking situations.
- b. To expose yourself to anxiety provoking situations
- c. To distract yourself so you can avoid thinking about the situation you are in.

Rate how certain you are with your answer?
- 1. I am guessing
- 2. I am pretty sure
- 3. I am fully confident

2. It can be good to consider what you can do to avoid getting depressed again even if you are not depressed right now and is confronted with challenges in life. Why?
- a. You will be prepared and will know how to handle challenging situations.
- b. Then you can avoid such situations as much as possible.
- c. Then you can prepare distractions when such situations occur.

(Continued)

Table 10.1 (Continued)

Rate how certain you are with your answer?
1. I am guessing
2. I am pretty sure
3. I am fully confident

The eating disorder test has not been published as a separate paper, but psychometric data for the weighted test showed an internal consistency of $\alpha = .62$, which is somewhat low but should be considered in relation to the need to measure different aspects of knowledge and not one single construct. Corresponding internal consistencies for other knowledge tests in other studies have been higher such as the depression test with Cronbach's $\alpha = .89$ (Andersson et al., 2023) and one recent knowledge test on loneliness with Cronbach's $\alpha = .87$ (Käll & Andersson, 2023). One test development paper on a knowledge test for adolescents was published by Berg, Andersson, and Rozental (2020). The final test included 20 items, and a factor analysis showed three factors: act in aversive states, using positive reinforcement and shifting attention. The internal consistency of this measure was Cronbach's $\alpha = .84$, and the test was later on used in a controlled trial (Berg, Rozental, de Brun Mangs, et al., 2020).

Effects in research

To my knowledge there is only one systematic review on the effects of digital treatments on knowledge acquisition (Jackson et al., 2023) which reported mostly good outcomes on knowledge tests. Overall the research studies I have been involved in (for example, the ones cited earlier on depression, eating disorders, anxiety in adolescents and loneliness) show increased knowledge when compared against control groups. Interestingly, in one study on adolescent depression, we found that pre-treatment knowledge was a negative predictor of outcome (Pearson's $r = -.38$), which suggests that we need to consider what our clients already know before we start treatment

(Berg et al., 2019). On the other hand, we have not replicated these findings in older samples, and in one study on eating disorders, it was reported that higher baseline knowledge levels predicted lower likelihood of dropout and a higher likelihood of adherence (Linardon et al., 2022). In line with what we have found, knowledge gains were not associated with treatment gains in that study. This may come as a surprise and disappointment, but I regarded as an advantage that explicit knowledge is not redundant or very closely related to the constructs we use to measure distress. In fact, I would argue that ICBT and CBT in general have knowledge gains as an important goal in itself that should be focused on more. Interestingly, in our depression trial on adults in which we collected two year follow-up data on knowledge test scores, we found that knowledge had decreased ($d = -0.72$), whereas symptom reductions remained stable (Andersson et al., 2023). Given the risk of relapse in depression, it could be the case that relapse prevention efforts should focus more on knowledge and how to maintain knowledge gains following treatment.

To date, research on knowledge and ICBT has not focused on attempts to influence knowledge acquisition, but in one controlled factorial design trial, we tested if it was possible to boost knowledge by using learning strategies (Berg, Rozental, de Brun Mangs, et al., 2020). The aim was to encourage a deeper processing and active retrieval of the treatment material. We did this by instructing the young adolescent participants to provide their own treatment summary, a quiz at the beginning of each module, applying treatment principles on fictive cases and also in their own life situation and also to explain what they just had experienced and read in the treatment to a significant other. They were also asked to relate the new knowledge to what they already knew about anxiety and CBT. Finally, in line with persuasive design, we added illustrative pictures, videos and treatment summaries. In the trial we could show that the added learning support led to larger improvements on a measure of anxiety ($d = 0.38$) and knowledge gain ($d = 0.42$).

Reflections

In contrast to much I refer to in this book, there is not much done on knowledge and CBT overall, and while there are studies in the field of internet interventions (Jackson et al., 2023), some have studied mental health literacy, and different measures have been used. This leads me to reflect upon the need for test development procedures as explicit knowledge is an important aspect of ICBT and differs between both treatments and conditions. It would also be good to have at least one measure of basic knowledge that can be complemented with more specific items. It is also useful to do qualitative studies as we have done on adolescents following ICBT (Berg, Malmqvist, et al., 2020), in which we identified two main themes. The first, named "Active agents of CBT", reflected a tendency to specifically remember and actively apply specific CBT principles in life. The second was named "Passive agents of CBT" and reflected a tendency to remember CBT treatment principles vaguely and express a passive or reactive usage of learned therapy content. Overall, and in light of what I wrote in Chapter 9 on persuasive design, the field of ICBT could benefit from measuring not only effects on symptoms but also how our different approaches to treatment delivery affect what the clients learn. Then explicit knowledge is just one aspect that lends itself to self-report measures, but, as reviewed in this chapter, there are other forms of knowledge and levels of knowledge that could be interesting to investigate in research.

11

How to develop new treatments

Developing ICBT programs can be done in many different ways. ICBT researchers can share material and even full treatment programs for translation and cultural adaption (see Chapter 13). This can speed up the dissemination of treatments as there is less need to train therapists in workshops, translate manuals and provide supervision as is the case in regular psychotherapy training and dissemination.

Another way to develop new treatments we have engaged in to a great extent in ICBT research is to take a program, say, for example, on depression for adults, and adapt them for another target groups like, for example, older adults. When going in the other direction from adults to adolescents, changes can be more striking in terms of examples, pictures used and even components like homework assignments and modules (with slightly different modules for adolescents). Such changes and adaptions may not be extensive but are still crucial to make the program more attractive and feasible. I do not have strong experimental support for this claim, but clinical experience suggests that this is the case at least for some target groups. One example is the work we have done on ICBT for patients with cardiovascular disease and comorbid symptoms of depression (Johansson et al., 2029), in which the treatment was adapted and involved information about cardiovascular disease as well as CBT techniques. Indeed, a qualitative study showed that "relevance and recognition" was a theme in the experiences reported by the research participants who had used the program (Lundgren et al., 2018). ICBT research has the potential to inform the whole

DOI: 10.4324/9781003453444-12

field of CBT as it is important to investigate how much a treatment should be adapted versus having transdiagnostic programs that do not mention the more specific problems the client may have. In the cardiovascular disease example, this would be a general CBT program with no modules or treatment material directly related to the disease. I will return to this topic later on in the book but want to mention it already here given the obvious fact that if treatments work more or less regardless of what kind of problems the person who receives it have (i.e., one size fits all), then much time would be saved. On the other hand, as mentioned, adaptions may sometimes be minor, and there is evidence that transdiagnostic protocols work for different target groups (Păsărelu et al., 2017). Indeed, treatments based on mindfulness is one example of a transdiagnostic treatment approach that can be helpful for different clients. During the pandemic we made alterations of our tailored ICBT program to fit the recommendations regarding Covid-19 (Aminoff et al., 2021), with for example, exposure recommendations in association with social anxiety adapted.

When we have a new idea

Sometimes a new idea pops up, and we decide to develop a new treatment program for a new target group for which no previous ICBT work has been done (at least not much). Early on we were much informed by previous research on self-help books, when we, for example, developed our first ICBT program for panic disorder (Carlbring et al., 2001). We then continued with other target groups, which will be covered later in the book, but after a series of programs (for example, on tinnitus, depression, chronic pain, social anxiety disorder, etc.), we came up with the idea to tailor the treatments based on client problems and preferences. As we had by that time several disorder-specific programs, we could "recycle" modules from these programs into a set of tailored modules that were adapted to be used for clients who may not have the disorder (like, for example, social anxiety disorder), but still can benefit from treatment modules on social anxiety. The number of modules has increased over the years but also inform development of new treatments. One example is the treatment of low self-esteem in adolescents which started with a module in the tailored treatment for adolescents with mixed anxiety and depression but then was made into a program on its own, which proved to be feasible (Berg et al., 2022). A similar early example was when a module on procrastination used in tailored ICBT for depression was expanded into a full treatment for that problem/condition (Rozental et al., 2015). I can give more examples, but the take-home message here is to learn from previous data/research, own experience and to use and adapt existing material.

There are of course hurdles and obstacles when developing treatments, but also possibilities. First, as commented on in Chapter 5, the treatment platform/technical solutions is crucial in ICBT. Some interesting ideas and treatment techniques used in face-to-face CBT may be hard to implement in the ICBT format, but this can also be the case for ideas regarding technical aspects. However, when developed, new technical solutions (like, for example, an insomnia diary with automatic calculations of sleep efficiency) can be re-used on later programs and trials. Aspects related to UX of the technical solution is another possible obstacle for innovation and development. It is not uncommon in the digital world to have technical problems, and standards may change from year to year.

Second, we have the issue of copyright. While common CBT techniques such as working with avoidance behaviours and exposure hardly can be "copyrighted" (but of course should be referenced correctly), there are treatment developers who may be hesitant to allow other researchers to use their published treatment material in an ICBT program. Within a research group we also need to be clear that no one is left behind who has contributed to the development. In my research group we often include students in our program development, but then also invite them as co-workers in studies. Some even end up doing their PhDs on the topic they did their Master's thesis on. Several different ways to handle this has been used over the years, but it is important to respect intellectual property and reference the material correctly.

Third, with regards to students, I also recommend that treatment program developers involve different generations when developing and designing treatments. I am constantly updated by my students, which can be crucial when working with younger clients in research. But it can also be important to involve senior persons who can assist, for example, by checking a program before it is tested with clients. I must admit that we have not been much focused over the years to engage in extensive co-design work before developing a treatment, with, for example, focus groups, stakeholder surveys, case studies, etc., before starting developing program. The literature on *complex interventions*, which ICBT programs can be viewed as, involve different levels to consider from techniques to policy, but also considering different perspectives (Skivington et al., 2021). Our approach, as mentioned earlier, has rather been to evaluate and obtain experiences from users of our programs, but this does not mean that the complexity of ICBT has been ignored, but rather that the development has been less formalized and much informed by earlier experiences. This means, for example, that the patient perspective for an upcoming trial is considered based on lessons learned from the previous trial and often also qualitative findings. It is often told that treatment development takes years. It is also often told that it is not possible to run controlled trials without much preparation and time. In ICBT research this is often not true in my and many of my international colleagues' experience. The internet changed the scene for treatment developers, and we have speeded up the process by running "pilot-RCTs", which are much more informative than small case series which was the standard (and still is) when developing face-to-face treatments. Said differently, if it is fairly easy to get research participants and the costs for running a controlled trial is marginally more than an open study, we prefer to do the first study as a controlled trial as we believe we learn more from those than open trials. On the other hand, the typical ICBT pilot-RCT is not smaller in terms of number of participants than many of the earlier face-to-face CBT trials, and arguably also of better quality (Schuster et al., 2021).

Fourth, and in some ways the most crucial hurdle, is the need for resources and funding. ICBT development has involved many sorts of funding from regular funding bodies to industry, but I also would like to add here more or less voluntary work with, for example, many of our trials having expert clinicians (for example, medical doctors) involved in the research as unpaid co-workers, students doing their theses in association with a trial, but also funding that may come from university contracts, hospitals, etc. There are huge differences in how costly ICBT development can be, with, for example, much money spent on platform and app development that, in too many cases, does not lead to a stable product and just disappears after the project period. Another source of costs can be participant fees for completing measures, which is very rare in, for example, Sweden and Australia but fairly common in research conducted in the United States. Overall, my impression is that ICBT research has been overall well supported by research funders (at least in comparison with psychotherapy research overall) but that much work also has been done with indirect funding and with data from regular clinical services.

Reflections

This chapter could be extended to almost a full book if the experiences of other treatment developers had been covered more and also different perspectives like the important work done by programmers/system developers. I have argued that ICBT and internet interventions in general have served as a vehicle for innovation and that much of what is new in psychotherapy research and in particular CBT comes from the ICBT world. Some may oppose and say that we are constantly re-inventing the wheel and that it is known since long that guided self-help (via different means) work. Against this I would argue that most psychotherapy research has been done in the Western world (in particular the US), with WEIRD (Western, Educated, Industrialized, Rich and Democratic) clients and that there are many psychological problems we do not know how to treat (I mentioned low self-esteem as an example) and target groups that have not been focused.

How to evaluate treatments

There are several constructs to measure when evaluating treatments overall, and in that respect ICBT is not different from other psychological treatments/psychotherapies. The main exception is that in-session behaviours in live sessions are not as relevant in remote treatments, but once an interaction between a client and a therapist starts (for example, via chat or video), it can be interesting to investigate that interaction and how it may affect treatment outcome. ICBT has a major advantage in that larger trials have been possible to conduct, and it is therefore not surprising that experts in other fields such as brain imaging and genetics have collaborated with ICBT researchers over the years. In this chapter I will first briefly review measures and outcomes used in ICBT research and then comment on different research designs and methods. I will return to measures and outcomes in subsequent chapters, and this will be an overview.

Measures and outcomes used

More or less all relevant contemporary self-report measures used in CBT research have their digital versions, and, as covered in Chapter 6, internet versions of self-report measures tend to work well and sometimes even better than the paper-and-pencil versions. The internet and smartphones also facilitate daily measures used in ecological momentary assessment (EMA) also mentioned in Chapter 6. One recommendation when planning a study or what to measure in clinical practice is to consider mixing established

DOI: 10.4324/9781003453444-13

"benchmark" measures with other more explorative measures if that is an interest. One example is research on the role of insight in ICBT for panic disorder, where we added measures of insight in the study but also measured more standard aspects of panic disorder (Halaj et al., 2023). There are numerous other examples with, for example, the research on knowledge acquisition measures covered in Chapter 10 and therapeutic alliance measures that will be mentioned in Chapter 16. Moreover, choice of measures are also influenced by target groups such as versions of depression measures related to age (for example, the Geriatric Depression Scale), but also, given the international context of ICBT research, whether measures have been properly translated and validated in the language they are used. Research studies often include numerous self-report measures that would not be feasible in clinical practice, and it is therefore an advantage if the core sets or outcomes used in research and clinical practice are the same. It is also an obvious advantage if the same measures can be used to evaluate the effects of different treatment formats as done in the large-scale "increasing access to psychological therapies" (IAPT) program in the United Kingdom (Clark, 2018). In particular, when it comes to self-report measures, these may involve not only clients but also partners and parents/ significant others of the clients and also measures for therapists and stakeholders like policymakers. Another important outcome that can be measured using self-report is the presence of negative effects of treatments (or adverse event). Several studies have measured this, and, while not common, negative effects can occur (Rozental et al., 2017) and should be measured both in research and in clinic.

While most outcome studies focus on validated self-report measures, there are also behavioural outcomes that can be measured both as pre-post changes, but also as process measures of how the program is used (for example, number of log-ins, questions asked to the therapist, etc.). Some studies have included actual tests of behaviour in structured test situations, with the behavioural approach task in specific phobia being one example (Andersson, Waara, et al., 2009). That test measures how close to a spider (in spider phobia) a client dares to be with a real live spider being the object. This form of behavioural test requires live testing, but, as mentioned in Chapter 6, sensors measuring, for example, sleep is possible to include as outcomes while not requiring live meetings. Overall, a vast majority of outcomes in ICBT research rely on self-report, but that is also the case for psychotherapy research in general.

Perhaps not classified as "behavioural", some studies have included tests of cognitive function as outcomes. In CBT research, tests of attention bias and selective memory are regarded as important. One example is a study we did where we measured future-directed thinking (with the future thinking task – a test of fluency of generating possible future events) before and after ICBT for depression (Andersson et al., 2013). We concluded that ICBT can lead to decreased negative future thinking and that changes in depression symptoms correlate to some extent with reductions in negative future thinking. Another example is research on attention modification in social anxiety disorder where we could not show any chance in attention bias (Boettcher et al., 2013).

Different biological measures/systems have also been used to some extent in association with ICBT research. There are, for example, a few studies on functional brain imaging, showing both functional and even structural changes following ICBT (Månsson, Carlbring, et al., 2013, 2017). Another interesting biological finding showed that cellular protection – telomere length and telomerase activity – was associated with improvement in ICBT for social anxiety disorder (Månsson et al., 2019). There are also studies on the role of genetics as predictors of treatment outcome showing conflicting findings, but with increasingly larger data sets, it is possible that role of genetics in treatment response will be further clarified (Boberg et al., 2023). There are other examples of biological measures such as heart rate being tested in association with ICBT trials (e.g., Morgan et al., 2009). Overall, ICBT research can be seen as a feasible venue for conducting larger studies on biological measures informed by a biopsychosocial approach to health. For the practising ICBT clinicians it will most likely be the measures that can be collected by the client in their phones (for example, physical activity monitoring), even if I do not know if that is used.

Speaking about a biopsychosocial approach to outcome measurements, there is a literature on societal outcomes and health economy in association with ICBT research (Kählke et al., 2022). This includes various outcomes related to, for example, work, health care consumption, treatment costs including development and many indirect outcomes such as willingness to pay for a treatment. This is a field on its own with special methods and assumptions, and it is recommended to work with experts when planning research or clinic audit monitoring (Drummond et al., 2005). The literature suggests that ICBT with guidance can be cost-effective but also that more research is needed (Kählke et al., 2022). One experience we had in my group when measuring costs was that it was rather demanding for participants to collect measures of costs and also for us to estimate indirect costs. But there are examples of health economy research that is more focused on health care costs and not covering a broader societal perspective which is easier to conduct (Mourad et al., 2022).

Overall, there researchers and clinicians need to carefully plan what to measure and how. It is a fine line between missing important variables to measure and overloading participants with tests and measures. In particular, in measurement intense trials, there is a risk that participants will focus less on the treatment and that measurement and treatment activities interact. In particular, my belief is that a control group in a trial with numerous measurement activities will get much more attention than the typical "treatment-as-usual" client and also that some self-report measures can be seen as providing information about what you as client is doing wrong. If, for example, stress measures are repeated every week, it can serve an indirect instruction that you need to do something about your life situation. And a Google search for "stress management" is not far away. In spite of this suspicion and results in trials showing that control groups reduce their symptoms (and do not get worse, as is wrongly assumed by some researchers outside of the field, referring to an assumed toxic effect of being on a waiting-list), we have not monitored carefully enough help-seeking activities in control groups which could explain this observation.

Research designs in ICBT research

Different research designs are used in ICBT studies. The most common in terms of publications is most likely the randomized controlled trial (RCT), which usually involves two or three groups that are compared. This is most likely explained by the comparable ease doing a controlled ICBT trial compared to traditional psychotherapy research. Guidelines on how to plan and conduct controlled trials can be consulted like the different versions of the CONSORT statement (e.g., Boutron et al., 2008). I mentioned the role of "pilot-RCT's" in the previous chapter, but open pre-post pilot studies are also published, and it is usually the only option when evaluating clinic outcomes. There is a distinction in clinical research between "efficacy studies" done in university or specialist settings versus "effectiveness/pragmatic studies", which basically means doing the research in ongoing existing clinical service and with "real-life" data. Both kinds of studies are published in ICBT research.

Even if RCTs are popular and widely used by researchers doing systematic reviews and meta-analyses (Andersson, Carlbring, Titov, et al., 2019), other research designs exist and are used. For example, case studies were popular when CBT was developed but are fairly rare in ICBT research (but see March et al., 2019 for an example). This is a pity as case studies can inform clinicians how a treatment works. I am not aware of any use of case-control designs (in which cases are matched against control participants) in ICBT research. Use of cluster randomized trial designs (when, for example, schools are randomized rather than individuals within schools) is, however, not uncommon (Abbott et al., 2009), even if they are much fewer than the standard RCT. In particular, in prevention research, cluster randomized designs can be feasible.

A more recent development in ICBT research is grounded in the need to discover "what works for whom" and what treatment components are needed. Given the larger samples possible in ICBT trials, use of factorial designs in which two or more independent variables are manipulated within the same study are increasingly used. This makes it possible to investigate main effects, for example,

65

of different ways to provide support and main effects of different kinds of treatment content, including if there are any interactions (Watkins & Newbold, 2020). Use of factorial designs is a logical next step when it is already known that a treatment works better than getting no treatment. Such ICBT trials are now being published (e.g., Berg, Rozental, de Brun Mangs, et al., 2020), with some showing statistically significant effects (like the one just mentioned showing a main effect of learning support in ICBT for adolescents). However, there are also factorial design trials with almost no main effects of the independent variables, which indicates that researchers need to study "strong" and "clinically relevant" independent variables (for example, if support on demand is as good as scheduled support), which can be informative even if there are no large differences. Factorial design trials can also study different outcome such as adherence and long-term effects (e.g., Andersson et al., 2023), as it may not be on just immediate symptom level where effects are seen. One challenge is that the same problem as with non-inferiority designs (showing that two treatments are equally effective) applies, namely a need for very large samples to secure enough statistical power to show equivalence or significant differences if effects are small. On the other hand, as with much intervention research now, trials that are well conducted with shared outcome measures can be used in systematic reviews and, in particular, individual patient data meta-analyses (IPDMA), which often have the power to study moderators of outcome in much larger samples (e.g., Karyotaki et al., 2018).

Another important way to do research is to focus on processes and investigate moderators and mediators of change, which has implications for research designs. Briefly, a mediating variable is assumed to explain the process (variance) between an independent variable and an outcome, whereas moderating variables influence the strength of a relationship between, say, a treatment and an outcome. Thus moderators can more or less always be checked using pre-treatment characteristics such as gender, whereas mediators require that the mediator and dependent variable are studied during the treatment process (Kazdin, 2007). Such studies can inform us about when a change occurs during a treatment and also show what is needed to obtain change. Studies on mediators of change require repeated measures of the change mechanism of interest, and there are several examples of ICBT studies investigating mediators of change. One example was a study testing moderated mediation in the treatment of irritable bowel syndrome (IBS), with two active treatments being compared (Ljótsson et al., 2013). Results showed that when exposure was introduced in the ICBT arm (in the middle of the treatment period), groups started to differ (with the other treatment being internet-based stress management).

Clinical research projects and indeed also clinical outcome auditing benefit from not only using quantitative outcomes and research procedures but also to incorporate qualitative research methods. There are several different approaches in qualitative research, ranging from content analyses of open data to more theoretically informed methods like discursive psychology and phenomenology. Most of the qualitative research in the field of ICBT use methods like thematic analysis (Braun & Clarke, 2021) and grounded theory (Strauss & Corbin, 1990), but this might be because most ICBT researchers have a background in quantitative methods, and therefore methods that are close to the data tend to be preferred. In any case, I strongly recommend mixed methods and that treatments are evaluated using both quantitative and qualitative research methods. I will return to research findings in qualitative studies on ICBT in Chapter 27.

Finally, with a look into the future, use of big data and machine learning approaches are likely to be more commonly used in ICBT research, in particular with data derived from regular clinics, as large data sets are preferred. This includes artificial intelligence and prediction research. I will return to this topic later on in this book.

Reflections

In this chapter I reviewed several ways to evaluate ICBT with some being very common among both researchers and clinicians (e.g., online questionnaires) and others being more rare in association with ICBT, such as online cognitive testing/neuropsychological tests, but also measures of knowledge. In clinical service settings there are other outcomes of interest such as number of clients assessed and then treated, uptake based on geographical location, etc. In research I also alluded to combined projects when, for example, a biological marker is investigated in relation to treatment outcome. I also briefly mentioned qualitative research that is increasingly used by ICBT researchers, both when developing and evaluating treatments. Finally, there is a totally different way to evaluate ICBT and, in particular, in the smartphone format in commercial settings, namely sales figures. This is not my area of expertise but highly relevant for private practice and also for dissemination of ICBT.

13

Adaptions and the role of culture

A challenge for therapists working with clients from different cultures is not only language but also cultural adaptation. In this chapter I will share our experiences of working both within (with immigrants) and outside my country Sweden with international collaborations in many places in the world (e.g., Romania).

One practical issue to consider is how technology works. As described in Chapter 5, the *Iterapi* platform is used in many different languages, which includes languages with different letters and going from right to left (e.g., Arabic). Not all systems support this, even if many do. Once implemented it can mean that a treatment programme is available in different languages for the client to choose. We usually start with the interface for which a template is used. The translation process of program content can be informed by digital tools such as Google Translate, but also other professional translation systems and increasingly artificial intelligence (for example, ChatGPT). However, I do believe that humans make a difference still, and therefore it is an advantage if the staff doing the translation comes from the same language and even cultural background. An early example of this was research from Australia with a Chinese-speaking population (Choi et al., 2012), in which the words used for depression had to be culturally adapted to low mood. The adaption was made by researchers with a dual Chinese/Australian background. Figure 13.1 presents an example of a screenshot from a transdiagnostic treatment in the Dari language.

Some researchers have described the process of cultural adaption including tools to facilitate the adaption. A cultural adaptation

DOI: 10.4324/9781003453444-14

Figure 13.1 Screenshot from a transdiagnostic treatment in Dari

should preferably be conducted in a structured and systematic way informed by adaptation guidelines. One example of the latter is the *Ecological Validity Framework* (Bernal et al., 1995), which involves eight components to consider when adapting interventions: language, persons (for example, patient-therapist), metaphors used, content presented, concepts used, goals, methods and finally the wider context in which the intervention is presented. Spanhel et al. (2021) did a systematic review on culturally adapted internet interventions and identified several components that had been considered in the literature such as values, mental health concepts and language tailoring, just to give three examples out of the 17 identified. Salamanca-Sanabria et al. (2019) did extensive work on cultural adaption of ICBT and incorporated different frameworks including principles from cross-cultural assessment research. They also presented a measure called the Cultural Relevance Questionnaire, which includes items to evaluate an intervention against. The measure has two sections, with the first being a general assessment of the programme and the second part an assessment of each of the included modules.

My impression is that researchers recently have focused more on the cultural aspects when adapting ICBT for new target groups, and also published on the process using mixed methodology (e.g., Demetry et al., 2023). In my earlier research, when we transferred programs to other settings and languages, it was common just to mention that the program was based on a previous program in another language. One example was a study on social anxiety disorder conducted in Romania in which our social anxiety disorder treatment was translated and adapted, but with no focus in the final paper on what cultural aspects had been adapted (Tulbure et al., 2015).

I mentioned here the role of culture, and that does not only apply with regards to ethnic groups but also other groups in society. There are, for example, several ICBT studies in which the treatment has been adapted to target specific groups of workers, like, for example, teachers (Ebert et al., 2014). Another example is when we adapted a depression treatment program based on religious beliefs (Tulbure et al., 2018). In that study we compared conventional cognitive behavioural therapy and religious CBT. While there were no differences between the two formats, we noted that the addition of religious components to CBT contributed to the initial treatment appeal for religious participants.

Later on in the book I will comment on ICBT programs for different age groups, which also relates to culture and different life situations (even if there are many similarities as well across different groups). Young persons may benefit from "age-specific" content, and the same goes for older persons. This is also relevant when providing psychological treatment for persons with somatic health problems. Within populations there may also be sub-groups such as sexual and ethnic minorities which can be reflected in programs when case examples are described.

Another way to adapt an intervention that has not received much attention, while probably being crucial, is to adapt interventions based on cognitive function. Years back we implemented two versions of modules in a study on depression, with one being longer and one being shorter and easier to read (Johansson et al., 2012). We did not focus more on this subsequently, but it is an aspect that deserves further investigation if we want to make it possible for persons with more limited cognitive resources to use a treatment program. There is a literature on reading levels and readability in relation to websites and also a few studies in which this has been checked in relation to ICBT programs (e.g., Gürses et al., 2023). There is a fine line between being too complicated and being viewed as superficial or even childish. Moreover, there are concepts used in CBT such as gradual exposure that need to be introduced, and if they are presented in lay non-technical terms, there is a risk that they can be misunderstood. Our clinical experience, however, is that text and other material should be easy to follow and understand, and one early solution we implemented was to provide extra material for clients in need of that or with an interest to know more.

The setting in which we have gained most experience of doing cultural adaptions has often been international collaborations. Typically, this starts with a research collaboration in which our *Iterapi* system is used, but the main responsible researchers are in the country where the participants are. I mentioned a study on social anxiety in Romania (Tulbure et al., 2015), but there are several other examples involving programs that are largely the same such as our tinnitus program that has been translated, adapted and used in Australia, Germany, United Kingdom, Unites States, including Spanish-speaking participants, Japan and Lithuania.

Reflections

I suspect that ICBT in different languages and with consideration of cultural aspects will become more common in the near future. In fact, many, if not most, countries have residents who may prefer to have their treatment in another language than the main language in the country, and some may even prefer, for example, English even if they speak the local language. Further, adaptions made on reading level and cognitive function may also increase. It is still the case that most research on ICBT has been done with Western populations and that there is a need to expand reach to get closer to the goal of providing global mental health. For example, the largest country in terms of population size in the world is now India, but there are, to my knowledge, not yet much ICBT research done there (for an example see Mehrotra et al., 2018).

14

Different ways to support

Internet treatments tend to work best when guidance is given, but there are various ways to do this and also examples of automated support and treatments with no human contact at all. In this chapter I will describe different kinds of support and how support can be given. I will cover different approaches and levels of support. Solutions such as "support on demand", which require less therapist time, will be covered. Further information on how to provide human support will be presented in Chapter 16 on therapist behaviours, in which I also cover the role or the therapeutic alliance.

Since the early start of internet interventions, the balance between reaching many clients when no support is given versus spending a significant amount of time with each client in order to reach the same treatment effects as in face-to-face CBT has been discussed and debated. In fact, it was brought up and discussed already during the first inaugural meeting of the *International Society for Research on Internet Interventions* in 2004. There were early examples of unguided treatments with massive and, in my opinion, unacceptable dropout rates. Farvolden et al. (2005) reported that only 12 (1.03%) out of 1161 registered users of their panic treatment completed the 12-week program. Similar experiences lead Eysenbach to formulate "the law of attrition" (Eysenbach, 2005), with the quote from the abstract: "What I call 'law of attrition' here is the observation that in any eHealth trial a substantial proportion of users drop out before completion or stop using the application." This unfortunately stuck in the field and gave internet interventions a bad reputation of always having high dropout rates. But internet treatments with

DOI: 10.4324/9781003453444-15

human support were tested with lower dropout rates, fairly often even not much more than in regular trials. In fact, we learned how to prevent dropout from both treatment and from assessments, but more on this later on. The important thing here is that unguided treatments initially seemed to both be associated with high dropout and potentially also smaller effects than treatments with at least some kind of human contact either before, during or after treatment (and often all of these), including a possibility to contact the researchers. Following the initial research and indeed some subsequent more or less "failed" trials on unguided treatments, researchers became much better, and there are now several studies on unguided treatments that work well by, for example, having some contact first, automated support functions and also security measures implemented (see Berger et al., 2011 for one early example). Moreover, we now face new technical solutions with artificial intelligence (AI), informing support and chatbots which, in one sense, are unguided but "mimic" the role of the human. Indeed, work by Titov and others have for long used *personalized automated messages*, and while clients may very well know that the text message was generated automatically, they still experience that support is given. Following an informative systematic review by Baumeister et al. (2014) and also an earlier review on depression (Andersson & Cuijpers, 2009), it has often been regarded as established that guided internet treatments work better than unguided ones. A more recent review confirmed this observation when comparing human versus technical support, with slightly better results for human guidance (d=0.11) and also better adherence (d=0.29) (Koelen et al., 2022). I must admit that this is a very scattered and complicated field to assess, and in an early review we noted that there might be a linear trend from no contact at all to much support, and that just any contact with a human may boost effects, with a Spearman correlation of .64 between degree of support and effect size in the depression trials we reviewed (Johansson & Andersson, 2012). My guess is that this might have changed with better automated support and also that there are major differences between different target groups, as, for example, adults with social anxiety disorder may be more likely to benefit from unguided treatments compared to, say, adolescents with symptoms of depression. Overall, unguided treatments remain an interesting and constantly changing topic.

The second format of support can be referred to as "support on demand" but has also been called *optional support* or *support on request*. I will use the term *support on demand*, which basically means that the clients are given the opportunity to ask questions and get support when they ask for it but will not get support scheduled if they do not ask for it. We came up with the idea to test if support on demand would work in a trial on social anxiety disorder back in 2010, but it took us many years to get it published (Käll et al., 2023). This is an interesting example of a study that ended up in the "file drawer", not because of the results but because of lack of time and focus. We were inspired by an early trial on computerized CBT for OCD, in which they had compared scheduled telephone support versus support on demand (Kenwright et al., 2005). To my knowledge there is just one systematic review on the difference between scheduled and support on demand, which showed no difference in terms of symptom reduction but better adherence with scheduled support (Koelen et al., 2022). The number of studies testing this is increasing, and more recent studies also show almost equivalent finds (see (Käll et al., 2023 for recent update). There are, however, indications that dropout rates increase slightly and also that some clients prefer scheduled support, but given the time and cost savings without sacrificing much of the effects, this support format should be further developed and tested. Indeed, providing customers with support when needed is a very common profession in, for example, retail business. Customers are used to being able to call for support when products fail, even if that has changed, as well with chatbots and automated support gradually replacing human support (which at least I find a bit annoying sometimes). While some support is possible to handle by the computer/artificial intelligence, it is an open question if all support can be handled that way. In the near future I can imagine a situation with stepped support, which, at least in clinical trials, often has been included as research participants have the right to contact the study team and also for security reasons. The reader may wonder what the difference is between self-guided and support on demand. I think the main difference is that in support on demand the client is encouraged to ask questions and ask for support, whereas in self-guided treatments that option is not made available. In other words, just knowing that you can get help if you need it may be beneficial. One estimate, however, is that clinicians need to spend about 10 times more time in scheduled support compared to support-on-demand.

A third support format, or rather way to categorize the support, is whether the support is given in an *asynchronous* manner (for example, via an email communication system) or if it is presented in *real time*. Starting with the first, this is the most commonly used support format in ICBT research and practice and has the advantage that the clinician and the client do not need to schedule a specific appointment for the contact. On the other hand, in trials we usually try to answer as soon as possible, at least during the work days. Asynchronous support also commonly includes being able to check the communication history before a response is given. Real-time text-based synchronous support – or chat sessions – can also be used to support clients. In our trials on adolescents we have noted that many in this target population liked this support form. Real-time text-based chat sessions is an example of a treatment form that is less well studied in research in relation to how much it has been practised. By definition, telephone and video support are also real-time support formats, and both have been used in ICBT research, and in particular the former. When we started with ICBT, we did not believe that e-mail support alone would be sufficient and therefore added scheduled phone calls in some of our early trials (e.g., on panic disorder, Carlbring et al., 2006). Now in 2024 we have had the possibility to use video chat in our Iterapi system for a long time, but interestingly we noted early that adolescents in a depression trial preferred to use text-only chat to a great extent over video chat (Topooco et al., 2018). In Chapter 8 I covered video therapy, and it is important to remind ourselves that this, following the Covid-19 pandemic, is now a very familiar way to access therapy, but distinctly different from ICBT in the self-help format.

A fourth and indeed fairly common way to provide support is *to blend face-to-face and ICBT components*. This is a rather scattered field as there is no obvious way to define how much of each format should be present (van der Vaart et al., 2014). Clinicians tend to favour a large proportion of face-to-face components, whereas in research trials the face-to-face part can be much less, and clients may also prefer a larger proportion of internet components. It is important that the two (or more) components are coherent. It is also important to decide if the face-to-face meetings should focus on supporting the self-help work, or if the self-help material rather supports the face-to-face work. There is a fairly large literature on blended treatments, and I was also part of a large European Community grant called "E-compared", in which blended treatments for depression were developed and tested. The pandemic also changed the scene for blended treatments that became much more common (e.g., blending video therapy and face-to-face). The blending I refer to here is rather the guided self-help (via computer or smartphone app) and face-to-face meetings. With regards to research support, it is clear that blended treatments work (Erbe et al., 2017), but it is not clear that blended treatments are better than email-guided ICBT and few studies showing equivalence with face-to-face CBT. My understanding of this is that blending can be necessary and should be part of services delivering ICBT. But it is also probably the case that there is a non-linear dose-response relationship between amount of support and effects, as we noted way back (Johansson & Andersson, 2012). As always, much more research is needed, and in particular research on more severe conditions that may require more face-to-face contact.

My last support format is distinctly different and not much investigated yet. It involves group support of clients either by peers or by a team of professionals. If we start with the first, we used online discussion forums as control groups in our early trials but also in combination with ICBT, and a few studies have also tested how well peer support of ICBT works (e.g., Tomasino et al., 2017). In this context it is also relevant to mention that there are several treatment protocols in which significant others are involved in the treatment, for example, ICBT for children. The second form of group support is, to my knowledge, largely unexplored, namely support from a team of professionals. Mehta et al. (2022) tested this support format against self-guided treatment and oddly reported that more participants in the self-guided versus team-guided condition showed clinically significant improvement on a measure of depression at post-treatment (76.5% vs 49.2%). Basically, team guidance involves more than one professional and is, in my experience, sometimes practised in routine ICBT care when, for example, a therapist is away for vacation. We have in my research group tested team-guided support on demand with support from different professionals. The results are not published yet but did not show the same inferiority as in the Mehta et al. (2022) study.

Reflections

In this chapter an overview of different support formats was presented, and, as with terminology overall, I am sorry that I cannot deliver a consensus on how to define support and also that the literature does not provide very clear answers. I am still convinced that there are benefits of human support and that we benefit from technology as well as the interpersonal context involved when support is given by a human (or even identified with name and picture). On the other hand, I also believe there are many clients who do not need us to support them and that pure self-help indeed can be helpful, in particular if you get interpersonal support elsewhere. Perhaps we should focus our research efforts on the question "who needs support?" in order to be better informed in our recommendations. The promising findings regarding support on demand mentioned in this chapter definitely need to be replicated as the cost savings (with much less therapist time needed) are substantial. On the other hand, in these studies there is still some contact with clinicians for diagnostic interviews, and that needs to be considered in line with our early findings that it might be the overall time with a human that is important and not just the time providing support.

15

The treatment process in research trials and in the clinic

In many presentations of how therapy works, the importance of referral and assessment procedures is not mentioned. In this chapter I will present how we usually run trials and also cover how ICBT can be delivered in regular clinical settings. There is an overlap between these two delivery settings, but also differences that may explain some of the discrepancies in the literature on, for example, dropout rates. Readers will hopefully recognize suggestions from earlier chapters in the book but also hear about some new perspectives.

A research trial

I start here with a typical research project. Research projects need funding, and that can take time and advanced guesswork. In some settings, like the one we have at my university, I have basic funding, and also students who do their MSc projects for six months by the end of a five-year clinical psychology program. A large proportion of our controlled trials are run together with these students who sometimes continue as PhD students later on. These PhD students more or less always also work in the trials as project managers, co-supervisors of MSC theses and also as clinical supervisors for the support part of the interventions. We also engage collaborators with special expertise when needed, such as medical doctors (e.g., psychiatrists) who assist in clinical decision making and join in as research collaborators. While projects funded by grant bodies are common, we can also run studies based on new ideas with existing

DOI: 10.4324/9781003453444-16

basic funding at low costs. This means we can test new research ideas more rapidly and, for example, run pilot RCTs before we are able to apply for funding. To get the funding can sometimes, in the best of worlds, take two years, but if some pilot work has been done it can strengthen an application. This is also made possible by having our Iterapi platform and a full-time webmaster/programmer with us. By taking advantage of existing material, it is often the case that, for example, outcome measures are already in place and do not need to be entered again, and we can also use existing treatment material to construct new treatments (see Chapter 11). Sometimes this can be a rapid process with new modules often written in association with the student projects and recycling of material, but it can also require substantial preparatory work with, for example, cultural adaption and translation of material. Sometimes we also develop totally new treatments.

Once we have decided on a research idea/topic and set up a research group for the study, we apply for ethics approval. In Sweden ethics application requires many documents but is rapidly handled, and we can get approval usually within two months. With regards to ethics I am aware of major differences between countries, from handling the application via the department to regulatory bodies for medical research with sometimes very long handling times. The ethics application is a useful exercise as decisions are made regarding just about everything in the study. Outcome measures, number of participants, consent forms, measurement occasions, and nowadays we also add that we will interview a selection of participants for a qualitative analysis (including an interview guide).

When we started doing ICBT studies in the late 1990s, studies had descriptive names such as "the panic project". Two MSc students who later went on and did their PhDs on ICBT came up with the idea to give a depression study a more attractive name. Hence, our first depression trial was called "David", which was an abbreviation for "depression treatment administered via the internet with discussion forum". This turned out to be a very good move as clients immediately referred to their participation as being part of the *David study*. Since then most of our studies have had specific names, and for some it has led to a series of studies, for example, the social anxiety disorder studies called *Sofie*, of which there are several. As I write this text the ongoing project name for the study we run right now is *Ines*, which is a study on transdiagnostic/transproblematic ICBT for mixed anxiety and depression. I could present a long list of study names used over the years. Most are not abbreviations, but rather good names that are not associated with products, famous persons, etc. Another ongoing study I am part of is called *Erica*, which is psychodynamic internet treatment for adolescents with symptoms of depression. We do not only use person names but also study names like Luna, Origo, Commit and Coronacope, just to give a few examples. I sometimes compare the study preparations with a "start-up"-company, as the whole process is much dependent on a well-functioning team of both new and experienced staff.

As soon as ethics has been cleared, the assessment and treatment set up and tested and other preparations made (like scheduling), we set a time for when to launch the study and begin recruitment. This is the most sensitive part of the study, and when it works best, it means starting mid-January (this is a time when more people search the internet for psychological problems – so called seasonality effect). There are different ways to "market" a study, for example, getting media attention (newspapers, radio and television), paying for advertisement in newspapers, but also social media, posters in hospitals and other settings like workplaces. Often the most effective way to recruit is via social media (Thornton et al., 2016), and with a bit of luck and contacts (for example, if we are promoted by an influencer), the recruitment can be very rapid.

Interested potential participants register on the study site and provide informed consent. They are then asked to complete the whole pre-treatment assessment battery. Based on the pre-treatment screening measures, we invite eligible participants for a structured telephone interview and have a calendar in the Iterapi system where they can choose a time to be interviewed. Persons who are deemed unsuitable for participation are either directly contacted and advised to seek other help or just contacted via the system and informed why the study is not suitable for them. The ones invited for interview have therefore already passed the first step. The interviews are usually held by the MSc students following training and can, for example, administer the MINI (Sheehan et al., 1998) psychiatric interview, but can also be arranged for the problem at hand if problems covered are not in the psychiatric domain. The next step is then to have intake meetings where all cases are presented, and a joint decision is made to include or exclude. Being clinically responsible as principal investigator, I take a lead in most of these intake meetings, which means that 1000s of client descriptions have passed my ears over the years. In order to speed up the process, we have the summary scores on the screen and spend less time if there are no concerns and a bit more if there are complicating factors (for example, regarding other treatment activities for other health problems). As one exclusion criteria is enough, there is no point in this setting to present all reasons for exclusion if the applicant has numerous reasons. This is, however, rare as the self-report screening handles most, and in a typical trial on adults, we may end up with only 10% being excluded following interview. When it comes to our studies on adolescents it is more complicated, and many more tend to be excluded. This is partly because of rapid changes that may occur for the adolescents, but also discrepancies between self-report and interview data. Once included, we inform the participants. We prefer to have all included participants randomized on one occasion. As we follow guidelines for running controlled trials, randomization is not done by a person working with the trial. We have in our platform a randomization function as well, which is the same thing as asking someone else to create a list. Sometimes we randomly allocate therapists to clients with the restriction that it is not a person who has been interviewed by the clinician. Stratification variables are rarely used unless we have a specific interest in a moderator and there are major size differences in subpopulations (for example, if one gender is much underrepresented).

Following randomization, treatment begins. We usually schedule supervision meetings for the clinicians who work in the trial. The clinical supervisor should be experienced in doing ICBT but may also be an expert in the specific field. For example, my own clinical experience of working with tinnitus patients made me a suitable clinical supervisor in a tinnitus trial done in Lithuania. This was an example of how we sometimes "export" our interventions to other settings and countries.

One aspect that is important to mention here is the role of time. A person who applies for participation in our trials will get a rapid response, and it can even be as short as two weeks between reporting interest and starting treatment. Thus the procedure is condensed compared to some clinical trials where it can take many weeks between the assessment and when treatment starts. Another aspect of time is what we call "the deadline effect". Participants are informed that we will assess outcome after, say, 10 weeks regardless of how much they have done in the treatment, and that deadline will also serve as a reminder to focus on the treatment. This is very similar to education when students study for an examination. If there is no deadline for a task, many of us will procrastinate and do something else instead. The role of the final telephone check-up call in ICBT studies, therefore, also serves as a deadline for completion. We investigated this years back in a study on unguided bibliotherapy for panic disorder in which we had a scheduled deadline and an interview after the treatment period (Nordin et al., 2010). In fact, the deadline effect can at least partly explain the large variation in adherence and effects seen in the studies on unguided ICBT. Some studies include a deadline and test session following unguided ICBT. I strongly recommend incorporating a deadline for the work, not only in studies but in the clinic as well. In fact, when there is no such deadline, we sometimes end up with many clients in the clinic who have not left but still are not active. Usually, therefore, clinical work requires some tidying and a deadline.

When a research trial ends and follow-up data are collected, it is time to write up the results and hopefully publish in a peer-reviewed scientific journal. As this is not a research methodology book, I will not go into detail about how to write scientific papers. However, it is often a good exercise to write up results and, for example, process data such as number of modules completed, time spent supporting clients, time clients have been logged in, etc. As mentioned in

Chapter 12, it is also useful to conduct open-ended semi-structured qualitative interviews to get feedback on how participants have experienced the treatment period and their therapist. Further, the write-up includes statistical analyses which involve understanding of outliers, dropouts and other aspects that are uncovered when data are analysed.

A research trial can generate more data if long-term follow-up results are collected. This needs to be stated in the ethics application. In controlled studies, when there is a control group that does not receive the active intervention, it is usually the case that they, by the time of the long-term follow-up (for example, one year later), have received the active intervention. It is still interesting to investigate the long-term results and also what participants recall from the intervention period.

In the clinic

The treatment process, including assessments in clinical settings, will differ from the research trial. The most common way to deliver CBT via modern information technology is most likely smartphone applications, but there are examples of clinical implementations for which service delivery models need to be created. A description of how ICBT has been implemented in routine care in five countries was made by Titov et al. (2018). This paper is interesting as it focused on successful clinics.

One clinic described was the internet psychiatry unit in Stockholm, Sweden, which I was involved in when it was initiated. As described in the paper, the clinic was set up within a specialist psychiatric care unit in 2007, but also in close association with the Karolinska Institute (medical university). Funding is still provided via the Swedish system of tax-funded health care, but clients also pay a small fee for the service, as is the case with all services (except for children). Clients can self-refer or be referred by, for example, psychiatrists and general practitioners. As in research studies, the process begins with online screening using validated questionnaires. Following this a face-to-face psychiatric assessment session is scheduled. Depending on the results clients are then assigned to a psychologist who will guide the client through the process of ICBT. The Stockholm clinic has several programs for problems like depression, social anxiety disorder, panic disorder, irritable bowel syndrome and insomnia. They also provide tailored treatment informed by client preferences and symptom profile (i.e., transproblematic). As in research trials, not all persons are suitable, and, for example, very severe conditions, high risk of suicide, language barriers or cognitive impairment may lead to a recommendation not to start ICBT and referral. The psychologist who handles the clients interacts with clients weekly via secure messages within the platform, SMS messages or, in some cases, telephone. Measures are collected on a weekly basis, and a built-in function can signal if the client deteriorates with regards to suicidal ideation. Following treatment, clients are interviewed and complete a more extensive post-treatment online assessment. Online assessment is also made three months post-treatment.

The MindSpot Clinic in Australia was another clinic described by Titov et al. (2018). I have been privileged to follow this clinic as external advisor, and it started in 2013. It is funded by the Australian Government and was launched by Macquarie University in Sydney. From the start this clinic has had a country-wide uptake in contrast to the internet psychiatry unit in Sweden which started with the Stockholm county region. The MindSpot Clinic has a triage system implemented, meaning that several tasks are performed including assessment, referral and treatment services (see Titov et al., 2017 for a description of the outcome after 30 months). Services are free for the clients, and a very large number of clients have been served over the years. Interestingly, many who access the assessments do not proceed to ICBT (about 1/5), which indicates that e-mental health services have an important role to serve in providing persons with assessment and feedback on the outcome. While the clinic focuses on anxiety and depression with transdiagnostic treatments delivered, they also have specific programs for clients with, for example, somatic disorders such as chronic pain. As with the internet psychiatry unit, many clients are self-referred. Measures are collected on a weekly basis in the ICBT programs (or courses as they call them) and also at three months post-treatment. The clinicians involved supporting clients and conducting interviews are registered mental health professionals (or in training). Another interesting aspect reported by Titov et al. (2018) is that the MindSpot Clinic clients can receive a hard copy of the ICBT programs via post.

Overall, these are two good examples of how ICBT can be implemented. There is not much written about the implementation process in relation to ICBT. This includes one of the earliest implementations we started on tinnitus treatment in Uppsala as early as 2000 and the Dutch Interapy services, which started even earlier as a research project and was implemented about the same time via insurance companies. A few words can be said about implementation research. The term implementation science is increasingly used to describe methods and strategies that facilitate the uptake of treatment including how novel interventions are transferred into regular use by practitioners and policymakers (Nilsen, 2015). This includes theories, models and frameworks used to describe and understand contextual factors that influence implementation. Implementation can be done in different stages, which has consequences for what kind of data to collect and analyse. For example, in the early stage, an intervention may appear very promising based on research and data from both clinicians and clients, but later data collected with other outcomes informed by implementation science can show that the new intervention (which, in our case, would be adding ICBT to existing services) may conflict with other goals and views of stakeholders and also when considering costs. One recent example of an implementation paper was a description of acceptance-oriented ICBT for chronic pain (Bendelin et al., 2024), highlighting both potentials and hurdles. From my perspective and given the fairly successful implementation of ICBT in Sweden often using programs we have developed in our research, I believe that implementation should be focused on more. For example, the collaboration between academia and real-life clinical settings is key for implementation of ICBT as so many decisions about implementation is based on research. But if clients and clinicians do not want a treatment, it matters less if there is research support, and therefore ICBT researchers have conducted stakeholder surveys to check how acceptable ICBT is for different target groups, for example, adolescents (Topooco et al., 2017).

Reflections

I mentioned in this chapter that research trials need to be checked for ethical approval, but ethics is not only something for research but also concerns all interventions. This has been written about in the literature (e.g., Dever Fitzgerald et al., 2010) but is a constantly changing matter. Now in 2024 we may, for example, need to consider ethical aspects of using AI. We may also need to more carefully consider studies reporting negative unwanted effects, as these are now more recognized (Rozental et al., 2014). Technical aspects such as data security are also relevant from an ethical point of view and consequences for third party (significant others). Much has happened since the first trial we did on headache back in 1998, and I hope some of the lessons learned have been conveyed in this chapter. I focused here on success stories, but there are several failed projects including studies with technical failures and large dropout numbers. But there are also failed and not seldom very costly implementation projects.

Part II

APPLICATIONS AND PRACTICE OF ICBT

Therapist behaviour and the role of the alliance

The role of the therapist can be crucial in ICBT, and here I will cover what therapists do when guiding clients in ICBT. I will also describe the role of the therapeutic alliance in ICBT and the function of supervision of ICBT clinicians in trials and in regular practice.

Much has been written about text communication between clients and their therapists in ICBT. As most ICBT protocols involve asynchronous interactions rather than real-time chats, a typical task for the therapist is to provide feedback on client e-mails/messages, including homework assignments. When responding to the client, there are things to consider. First, language needs to be understandable and empathic. Then a major task is to support and reinforce progress, including pointers to upcoming work. It can also include providing clarifications. When we did one of the first studies on therapist behaviours in ICBT, we noted eight categories of responses, of which task reinforcement, alliance bolstering, task prompting, psychoeducation, self-efficacy shaping and empathetic utterance were expected ones (Paxling et al., 2013). But therapists also engaged in some self-disclosure (when appropriate) and, finally, something we named deadline flexibility. The last category was actually found to be not so feasible as a negative correlation with outcome was noted ($r = -.37$). This association cannot be regarded as causal as clients who show poor adherence to the treatment are more likely to generate supportive and understanding responses from their therapist. There are more studies along the same line suggesting that what the therapist writes in correspondence makes a difference. In one fairly recent study by Hadjistavropoulos et al. (2019), the focus was on undesirable behaviours exhibited by therapists in their correspondence with patients. They developed a scale called the Undesirable Therapist Behaviour Scale and analysed emails sent from therapists to clients. They found several examples of undesirable behaviours that were infrequent, such as inadequate detail, unaddressed content, unsupportive tone, missed correspondence, inappropriate self-disclosure and unmanaged risk. Interestingly, they found at least one undesirable behaviour in as many as 11% of the emails, and many clients had received at least one email containing undesirable therapist behaviour (37%). This study again supports the notion that what we write to our clients in emails can make a difference. There are also a few studies on other aspects of the client-therapist interactions. Soucy et al. (2019) coded questions clients ask during treatment. Many questions concerned assistance to enhance understanding and apply the recommendations presented in the program (46.72% of the questions asked). But questions were also asked about the therapeutic process (22.62%), technical challenges (18.25%) and help with other problems not covered in the program (12.41%).

In clinical trials and in training of novice therapists, we usually give examples of common ways to respond and also provide supervision in trials to advice on how to handle more difficult situations such as aggression (very rare) and poor compliance (very common). I also give workshops and then let participants practice how to respond to client emails. Among the advice given is to focus on positive reinforcement and progress when clients have not managed to complete homework as planned or just parts of it. Another advice is to refer to past and future material in the treatment program. For example, it can be a good idea to suggest: "It can be useful to go back to earlier modules and repeat as we tend to forget sometimes" and as stated in this quote:

> The problem you mention will be addressed later on in the upcoming module in two weeks. I hope you can benefit from the work in the module you work with right now, as it is intended to prepare you for the later work.

It is not advisable to invite clients to a conversation like asking "Tell me more", with the exception of crisis management for which it may be required to call the client. Otherwise it is not a good idea to start a conversation as it can distract from the program and is not likely to benefit the client. Indeed, the role of scheduled real-time sessions in ICBT as adjunct to the email correspondence did not add anything in a trial on adolescents with mixed anxiety and depression (Berg, Rozental, de Brun Mangs, et al., 2020). However, this is a not a strict recommendation, and there are definitely clients who benefit from more intense therapist contact just as there are others who do not need any contact at all.

Therapeutic alliance

A topic related to therapist behaviours is the concept of *therapeutic or working alliance*. This is one of the most studied aspects of psychotherapy and is also widely regarded as important in CBT. Fairly early ICBT researchers adapted the commonly used Working Alliance Inventory for use in ICBT trials, and there are now several studies in which early alliance (defined as agreement on *tasks, goals and the bond* between the therapist and the client) has been correlated with treatment outcome. Results have varied from no significant correlations to about the same as in face-to-face CBT. In one comprehensive overview on the role of the alliance in ICBT, Berger (2017) highlighted the importance of not only considering the alliance with the therapist but also with the program. He also noted that overall alliance ratings tended to be high in internet interventions trials. In one recent comprehensive systematic review of predictors and moderators of outcome in ICBT, Haller et al. (2023) concluded that a better working alliance predicted better treatment outcome in almost all studies reviewed, in line with several reviews on this topic (e.g., Kaiser et al., 2021). In fact, the average correlation between early alliance and outcome reported by Kaiser et al. ($r = 0.20$), is surprisingly similar to what has been found in face-to-face psychotherapy. But it should again be mentioned that there are studies reporting no association. While this topic has been studied many times, there is more to do. For example, one study from Israel showed that client alliance with the program predicted treatment outcomes, whereas alliance with the therapist predicted adherence in ICBT for panic disorder (Zalaznik et al., 2021). A study from Canada reported that the coded therapist behaviours questionnaire feedback and task reinforcement were associated with higher client ratings of therapeutic alliance (Schneider et al., 2016). This research is highly relevant when there is a therapist supporting the client. But much ICBT is done without a therapist, and it could also be questioned what kind of alliance we measure when the actual contact with the client (in terms of content in emails) can be very limited and far from the situation when we have the client in the room. Therefore the notion to study alliance with the program makes sense, but also to adapt alliance measures for ICBT as has been done many times. We also face an era with avatars (Heim et al., 2018) and alliance with a non-human supporter mimicking the therapist role.

Reflections

Guiding a client in a self-help treatment can be very rewarding, and a good relationship can be established just as in face-to-face CBT. On reflection this is not so strange. A client in ICBT can return to the correspondence and get support in a more reliable way than a client remembering what the therapist said several weeks back. Also sometimes a few supportive good words can be very effective, whereas in face-to-face treatment, so much else goes on ("Was it hard to find a parking place today?"). On the other hand, what we gain in asynchronous personalized test support is, at least for some clients, not a as powerful as when you see your therapist with a happy face when you report about your progress. But if a therapist has had a bad day, that will be more noticed as well, and to quote Isaac Marks "computers have no eyebrows". It might very well be that the lack of difference in effects between guided

ICBT and face-to-face therapy (Hedman-Lagerlöf et al., 2023) can be explained by the two formats handling different aspects of the therapy process. To date, we have not been able to prove that in research, but perhaps with larger data sets we will be able to detect what works for whom. Finally, it will be interesting to see what will happen with automated and AI-informed therapy, and it might very well be that some clients will prefer an avatar (or similar solutions), whereas other clients AND therapists will prefer a real person with a name providing the support.

17

Internet treatments for anxiety: Children and adolescents

In this and the nine following chapters I will summarize how ICBT has been adapted and tested for different target groups. I will start with a short description of the groups and then cover a selection of treatments tested, including adaptions and challenges we have had when doing research. I will give examples of programs and studies/ reviews, but it is not possible to cover everything (as it would make this book twice as long just because of the much longer reference list!). I will end with some reflections.

The target groups

There are not as many programs and trials on anxiety in children and adolescents as there are for adults. Another important consideration is the transdiagnostic character of symptoms, making it harder to stick to one diagnosis in a trial/program. There are also very few studies on anxiety in children aged 12 years or younger, for whom parents need to be involved in the treatment. When it comes to adolescents with anxiety disorders, we have focused our research on the age range 15–19 years. When it comes to adolescents, large differences in how mature they are may be present, in the sense that a 15-year-old client can be more mature and able to do ICBT than another adolescent aged 18 years. Apart from the mixed anxiety/depression/poor self-esteem character of adolescent anxiety, research programs and research studies have been done on social anxiety disorder, specific phobia, obsessive-compulsive disorder

DOI: 10.4324/9781003453444-19

(covered here but no longer regarded as an anxiety disorder) and body dysmorphic disorder. Some programs are better described as "blended treatments" I referred to earlier, as in-vivo sessions are included. While there is research on trauma-focused CBT for adolescents, I have not seen much of this in the ICBT literature. In fact, when it comes to more "severe" conditions, legal and ethical considerations can at least partly explain why there is much less work on adolescents and children.

In a fairly recent systematic review on ICBT for anxiety disorders in children and adolescents, the authors could only include nine controlled trials (Cervin & Lundgren, 2022). Among the conditions included were generalized anxiety disorder, social anxiety disorder, separation anxiety disorder and specific phobia. Their review did not cover OCD. In an earlier review by Vigerland, Lenhard, et al. (2016) on ICBT for children and adolescents, which also included open studies, as few as seven studies were included, with one additional on OCD. In fact, few research groups have been involved, and while I worked with researchers in Stockholm when they started (e.g., Vigerland, Ljótsson, et al., 2016), and did early work here in my own university (Silfvernagel et al., 2015), we later moved on to treatments in which anxiety and other symptoms as depression were targeted in transdiagnostic treatment (Berg, Rozental, de Brun Mangs, et al., 2020). Given the relative lack of research and implementations of ICBT for anxiety in younger target groups, a consensus report was published providing recommendations on how to move the field forward (Hill et al., 2018).

When it comes to treatment contents it should be acknowledged that while CBT principles apply, they need to be presented in a manner that suits children (for example, for clients aged 8–12 years) or adolescents. Thus gamification principles, pictures and adapted language and examples are crucial. Further, having a platform that can be accessed via the smartphone (see Chapter 5 on responsive formats) is key when working with the target group. CBT for anxiety relies heavily on exposure principles, and ICBT is no exception. Interestingly, in our experience, adolescents much appreciate working with thoughts, and therefore cognitive therapy techniques are very useful as well. I will later comment on our finding that many of our adolescent participants reported problems with poor self-esteem, which led us to develop a program focusing on that problem (see Chapter 24). Parent involvement is necessary for children and can be an advantage for adolescents as well, but perhaps not as much. In fact, for some adolescents it can even be an advantage that parents are not involved, at least if they are 15 years or older and mature enough to understand the concepts and rationale behind ICBT.

The evidence

As a consequence of the relatively few studies, the evidence base is less well developed for children and adolescents with anxiety disorders than it is for adults. On the other hand, there are convincing studies suggesting that guided ICBT can be effective compared to attention control (Nordh et al., 2021) and even face-to-face CBT (Spence et al., 2011). This tentative conclusion is also supported by the systematic reviews mentioned earlier (Cervin & Lundgren, 2022; Vigerland, Lenhard, et al., 2016). There are also controlled studies on OCD (e.g., Lenhard et al., 2017), but it is striking that so few studies have been published on younger children with anxiety (Vigerland, Ljótsson, et al., 2016 and McLellan et al., 2024 are two exceptions). One development we initiated was covered in Chapter 10, namely boosting the effects of ICBT by considering educational science (Berg, Rozental, de Brun Mangs, et al., 2020). While this is just one study, it would be interesting to know more about the role of knowledge acquisition in ICBT for adolescents and children with anxiety, and in particular the long-term effects, as these young persons get older and may develop anxiety disorders as adults.

Reflections

I must admit that running trials on adolescents is exciting but also a bit scary as changes can occur so rapidly. We are always very careful to be available to support our adolescent clients via telephone if a crisis should occur. On the other hand, and fortunately more common, rapid improvements are seen, which can be a challenge in a study as the young client then can be less motivated to continue therapy. As mentioned, the role of significant others and, in this case, parents can be very important. It is fairly common in our trials that a parent or another adult has recommended the study, but also that the young person locates the study on social media. One anecdote is when my students suggested that we should advertise an upcoming trial on Snapchat, and I as senior researcher hardly knew about the platform (this was a few years back). It worked well. The Snapchat story also illustrates the importance of having a team with younger co-workers (students), as they are much closer to the target population in age and may also have siblings that can assist and check the contents in terms of language and appearance. I will comment more on this in the chapter on depression treatments for adolescents. While we have had boys in our trials, they are very few, which, to some extent, mirrors the epidemiological studies on anxiety in adolescents but most likely also societal expectations, with women being more interested in psychology/awareness of emotions and also mature enough to be able to be a research participant in a trial.

Another reflection I will return to is how much ICBT has been implemented. There are, to my knowledge, much less done here as well when it comes to adolescents with anxiety disorders (Hill et al., 2018), and even less when it comes to younger children and their parents. It is interesting to follow how ICBT can be implemented in rural areas, and there are a few examples with a Swedish study reporting on children with anxiety (Jolstedt et al., 2018).

18

Internet treatments for anxiety: Adults

Anxiety disorders in adults were targeted early in the history of ICBT, with researchers in Australia and we in Sweden being among the first focusing on panic disorder (Andersson, 2018). At the same time researchers in the Netherlands started to do research on traumatic experiences and PTSD (which I cover here even if it is separated in the DSM-5 manual). Following these initial steps, the field grew rapidly.

Target groups and programs

More or less all common adult anxiety disorder diagnoses in the *Diagnostic and Statistical Manual of Mental Disorders – DSM-5* (American Psychiatric Association, 2013) – have been the topic of ICBT programs and research. These include panic disorder, agoraphobia, social anxiety disorder, generalized anxiety disorder and specific phobia. I also mention here what was formerly known as hypochondriasis – illness anxiety disorder – which is classified as a somatic symptom and related disorder, but very close to the anxiety disorders in terms of overlap. In addition, obsessive-compulsive disorder (OCD) will be mentioned here as well as post-traumatic stress disorder (PTSD). It is not always helpful for a CBT clinician to only consider the diagnostic categories in the DSM, as overlap between symptoms and diagnoses is more or less always present at some point (in particular the link between mood and anxiety disorders). However, when following the diagnostic criteria for a

DOI: 10.4324/9781003453444-20

disorder like social anxiety disorder with diagnostic interviews, and inclusion of diagnosed participants, guided ICBT programs have repeatedly been found to work (Andersson, Carlbring, Titov, et al., 2019). In other words, diagnosis-specific programs can be very effective, even if we as researchers need to test how specific they are and consider transdiagnostic approaches as there is also much overlap between treatment protocols for different disorders.

The target group "anxiety disorders in adults" is very broad, which is also reflected in the literature. For a start, much ICBT research suffers from the WEIRD problem mentioned in Chapter 11 (Western, Educated, Industrialized, Rich and Democratic), and this is not unique for ICBT research, but rather a common observation in psychotherapy research and indeed research in general. Fortunately, an increasing number of programs are tested in other settings, for example, ICBT for social anxiety disorder in Romania (Tulbure et al., 2015). One way to handle the WEIRD problem is to document effects in real clinical settings, in so-called effectiveness/pragmatic studies I have briefly mentioned earlier in this book. I will comment on this here as well when reviewing the evidence. While there are not as many trials on direct comparisons between ICBT and face-to-face CBT, the largest ones have been done on anxiety disorders in adults, and that is of course an important aspect to consider when evaluating the research support (Hedman-Lagerlöf et al., 2023).

As there is so much research and many programs, I need to comment briefly on treatment contents. As many readers know very well, CBT is not a "technique", but rather a broad range of theoretical assumptions, techniques and procedures that fall under the umbrella term CBT. This is of course reflected in the ICBT literature as well. Most ICBT protocols include both cognitive and behavioural techniques, including emotion regulation, but there are also less obvious bodily oriented methods like applied relaxation and mindfulness that are included in some programs and even as stand-alone internet interventions. Added to that we have acceptance and commitment therapy, which I regard as a form of CBT but will comment on a bit more in Chapter 26, where are I also cover mindfulness. Having said that, there are many shared features as mentioned earlier in this book, with psychoeducation, rationale, exercises, homework assignments and feedback (when guidance is given) being defining features of CBT.

The evidence

My approach here will be to review the literature in the style of an "umbrella review". Umbrella reviews are only possible to conduct in fields where many meta-analyses are published. As there are many controlled trials, new meta-analyses appear on ICBT constantly, calling for umbrella reviews to get an overview of the evidence. To my knowledge we were among the first to do an umbrella review of ICBT (Andersson, Carlbring, Titov, et al., 2019), but focused on anxiety and mood disorders. For readers less familiar with meta-analyses, it can be good to know that a between group of 0.20 is regarded as small, 0.50 as moderate and 0.80 as large (different metrics are stated, but they are standardized mean differences). The usual control groups are either waiting lists or active controls (for example, treatment as usual), but there are also direct comparisons of treatments, and then effects usually tend to be much smaller. But the interpretation is about the same as stated earlier. There are also sometimes meta-analyses that report within-group effects using similar metrics (e.g., Cohen's d). These should be interpreted with more caution as larger within-group effects are usually found compared to between-group effects.

Starting with *panic disorder*, I found one meta-analysis which included 16 controlled trials and reported a large between group effect (Hedge's $g = 1.15$), based on 1015 trial participants (Domhardt et al., 2020). In the same meta-analysis they reported results on symptoms of agoraphobia ($g = 1.15$), as well as comparisons between active control conditions mirroring previous reviews with insignificant differences against face-to-face. Interestingly, these results are surprisingly similar to the ones we reported more than 20 years ago (Carlbring et al., 2001).

Social anxiety disorder has been the topic of much ICBT research, with a recent study by Clark et al. (2023) being a major contribution suggesting equal effects of ICBT and face-to-face CBT. The most recent meta-analytic review by Guo et al. (2021) included 20 studies with 1743 participants and reported a moderate effect against control conditions of $g = 0.55$. The effect was larger when the comparison was waiting list conditions ($g = 0.79$). In addition to immediate effects, long-term effects as long as five years post-treatment have been reported (Andersson et al., 2018).

Generalized anxiety disorder is sometimes regarded as more difficult to treat than other anxiety disorders, but there are several controlled trials on different forms of ICBT. The most recent meta-analysis (Eilert et al., 2021) included 20 studies with a total of 1178 participants, and reported a large between group effect ($g = 0.79$) in comparison with controls.

Specific phobia has been less in focus of ICBT research, and a meta-analysis focusing on both internet and mobile phone interventions could only include five controlled and four uncontrolled trials (Mor et al., 2021). The review focused on within-group effects, and an effect of $g = 1.15$ was reported.

Illness anxiety disorder, which is also called health anxiety, has been studied in a few controlled ICBT trials. I found one meta-analysis (Axelsson & Hedman-Lagerlöf, 2019) which reported a large between-group effect on health anxiety measures ($g = 1.09$) based on four trials.

Obsessive-compulsive disorder (OCD) can be mentioned here as well, and there are both programs and controlled trials suggesting that guided ICBT using exposure and response prevention works. I located one recent meta-analysis (Machado-Sousa et al., 2023) which included 15 studies (N = 522), out of which six were randomized controlled trials. The findings showed large effect sizes of ICBT in improving OCD symptoms in pre to post ($g = 1.14$), pre to follow-up ($g = 1.16$) and between control and experimental groups ($g = 0.81$). I mention here that there are also a few trials on body dysmorphic disorder (e.g., Enander et al., 2016).

Post-traumatic stress disorder (PTSD) is another major problem for which much ICBT research has been done, starting with the early work in the Netherlands on a program called Interapy (Lange et al., 2001). For PTSD there have been updates of a Cochrane Review, but the group behind that review also reported a meta-analysis (Lewis et al., 2019). That review analysed 10 studies including 720 participants. The effects against waitlist were (SMD = -0.60), which is a moderate effect. Larger effects and also including an active control condition was reported more recently by Ehlers et al. (2023). Another important and well-done trial compared ICBT against face-to-face treatment with almost 200 participants and reported non-inferiority (Bisson et al., 2022).

Reflections

I promised to mention effectiveness/pragmatic studies, and there are several published on most of the diagnoses I covered in this chapter (see Etzelmueller et al., 2020 for a recent review). I mentioned earlier in the chapter the most recent review on direct comparisons between face-to-face and guided ICBT (Hedman-Lagerlöf et al., 2023), and among the 31 trials included in that review, 12 studies had the diagnoses covered in this chapter as target groups. It is interesting to note that the field has largely moved on from diagnosis-specific treatments to more transdiagnostic or tailored approaches covered later in this book. One reason for us to do this was the need to exclude many participants from diagnosis-specific trials on, for example, panic disorder, as they had anxiety and indeed panic attacks but did not fulfil the diagnostic criteria for a panic disorder. On the other hand, in the trials covering a broader range of clients, diagnostic interviews are often implemented which provide information on how well ICBT works for the specific diagnoses as well but also considering the substantial comorbidity.

19

Internet treatments for anxiety: Older adults

Anxiety disorders are also common among older persons, but there has been much less research focusing on this group (usually defined as being 60 or 65 years and older). Older persons are usually not excluded from studies on adults reviewed in the previous chapter. Indeed, a clinical observation I have made in our more recent trials is that older adults more often report interest and are included, even as old as 80 years. But there is still a need to consider ICBT programs designed for older adults and the effects. Earlier on there was a digital divide, with older persons sometimes being less well oriented in the use of information technology. But in modern society today (in particular Sweden), it is almost impossible to live an independent life without using digital solutions, with, for example, money and bank affairs requiring use of computers and/or smartphones. Moreover, older adults in 2024 have lived with close to 30 years of internet use, which means that they were at least middle aged when the internet appeared in society. ICBT for older adults with anxiety started around 2010 with researchers in Australia, and we in Sweden followed a few years later.

Target groups and programs

To my knowledge most programs and studies on older adults with anxiety disorders have not focused on one diagnosis and treatment, but rather either transdiagnostic or tailored approaches. Some studies

DOI: 10.4324/9781003453444-21

have reported clinical data suggesting that ICBT is both effective and acceptable for older adults (Mewton et al., 2013), and this is my impression as well even if we only have done one controlled trial focused on anxiety disorders which also considered symptoms of depression (Silfvernagel et al., 2018). More studies with older adults have been done on depression (see Chapter 22) and on somatic disorders in which older adults are well represented (e.g., heart failure patients). I mentioned in Chapter 13 that programs for older adults may need to be adapted for the age group just as we do for adolescents when having a program originally aimed for adults. This is not only a question of examples and choice of illustrations but can also concern technical matters such as problems logging in.

The evidence

Given the relative lack of controlled trials with a focus on anxiety disorders in older adults, I could only find reviews that had a broader focus. One systematic review included only three controlled trials and reported an average Hedges' g of 0.90 (Dworschak et al., 2022), which was not statistically significant but in line with other studies in the field. One of the trials included were on older adults with generalized anxiety disorder showing a large between-group effect of $d = 0.85$ (Jones et al., 2016). In our own trial, we used an online version of the Wisconsin Card Sorting Test (measuring perseverative errors) at pre-treatment and reported a significant correlation between perseverative errors and anxiety outcome ($r = -.45$), indicating that cognitive function was associated with poorer outcomes (Silfvernagel et al., 2018). As mentioned, clinical data support the notion that ICBT for anxiety can work for older adults (Mewton et al., 2013), and overall we could investigate effects by analysing existing data to check if included persons older than 60 benefit from ICBT (with so-called individual patient data meta-analyses). I should also mention here that there is at least one trial on PTSD in older adults who had experienced childhood trauma (Knaevelsrud et al., 2017). That trial included 94 participants, and a between-group effect of $d = 0.42$ was reported in favour of the treatment.

Reflections

As with younger persons, there may be major differences within the group of older adults in terms of cognitive ageing and use of technology and, in the case of older persons, the high likelihood of having comorbid chronic medical conditions. Related to medical conditions is the fact that many older persons are on medications, may be survivors of cancer or heart disease and have hearing or vision impairment. Moreover, a substantial proportion of older persons may also care for a partner or an adult child (with, for example, intellectual disability), making it hard to engage in ICBT homework that requires leaving home. Another aspect is the clients' financial situation even if many participants in research trials tend to be both well educated and not poor. In spite of these possible hurdles it is more typical that older persons are motivated and engaged. For some, anxiety may have been part of their whole life, whereas for others it might become a problem in association with life changes such as retirement, bereavement and illness.

20

Internet treatments for depression: Children and adolescents

The first episode of major depression often occurs in young adolescent women, and it is therefore important to provide treatment, not only to reduce symptoms but also to prepare and prevent for future episodes of depression in adulthood. When it comes to younger children I am not aware of any ICBT work done on depression, and the chapter will therefore focus on the work done on symptoms of depression and major depressive disorder in adolescents (usually aged 15–19 years).

Target groups and programs

The target group is dominated by young women, and while adolescent boys also may experience symptoms of depression, they have been rare in most studies. In fact, even if depression is at least twice as common among young women and the earlier puberty makes a difference, it is not uncommon to have more than 90% of women in ICBT trials on adolescents. It is also a known fact that comorbidity is common when it comes to depression, and in particular with the anxiety disorders. Early onset depression has negative consequences in many life domains such as education, peer and romantic relations, family and general health, just to mention a few examples. In our experience it is also the case that adolescents may not recognize and understand their problems in terms of depression. For example, I will mention later in this book our work on poor

DOI: 10.4324/9781003453444-22

self-esteem which originated from what our adolescent participants told us in interviews when running depression trials.

When it comes to programs, there have been several tested, with early ones being more focused on prevention and later studies on major depression, or at least significant symptoms of depression. Most programs have been based on CBT, including the common treatment components psychoeducation, behavioural activation and cognitive work, and also common is emotion regulation strategies and relapse prevention advice. It can be mentioned again that ICBT programs need to be adapted for the target group, and for adolescents this was crucial when we adapted a program for adults (Topooco et al., 2018). Programs for depression in adolescents have also varied the therapist support, from unguided treatments (which, for this target group, often has led to substantial dropout and perhaps also smaller effects) to treatments where real-time support is given in chat sessions. The usual format of asynchronous e-mail support is also common in ICBT research on adolescents. Figure 20.1 is a screenshot from an ICBT program for adolescents with mixed anxiety and depression.

The evidence

In contrast to the fewer studies on anxiety disorders in adolescents, there are more controlled trials and also meta-analyses on ICBT for adolescents with depression and symptoms of depression. One recent meta-analysis included 18 controlled trials involving 1683 clients (Wu et al., 2023). They reported an average between-group effect size of SMD = 0.42, but that was when pooling different comparison groups and support formats. As often is the case, effects were larger when comparing against waiting-list controls, but the review did not provide an accurate picture of the research (errors in coding studies). Overall, the earlier meta-analysis by Ebert et al. (2015) provided a more accurate picture with an overall effect size of $g = 0.76$), even if that review was based on fewer studies. It is

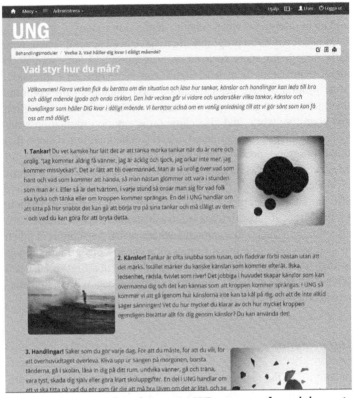

Figure 20.1 Screenshot from an ICBT program for adolescents with mixed anxiety and depression

not surprising to find conflicting results in systematic reviews when treatments have been inconsistently defined as well as different support formats have been tested. In addition, other influencing factors such as having much interaction with the research staff during assessment and outcome monitoring can influence, even if the treatment later is defined as "unguided". I could not locate any studies directly comparing ICBT versus face-to-face CBT for adolescents with depression, and perhaps more important is the relative lack of long-term follow-up studies to support the notion that treatment of depression is beneficial in the long run, as has been done for adults (Andersson et al., 2018).

Reflections

Our studies on ICBT for adolescents with symptoms of depression have been very informative and inspiring. For a start we had to exclude many clients who reported interest. This was either because of having too few symptoms or having too severe problems and concurrent treatments that needed to be handled first. The clients in our trials have differed markedly, with some being more "psychiatric" in the sense that they have a history of child psychiatry clinics and medications, whereas for others it can be the first time ever they seek help for psychological problems. As I mentioned in the chapter on anxiety disorders in adolescents, parental involvement may also differ. Trends in diagnosing and also how clients describe their problems can vary over time as well, with, for example, neuropsychiatric conditions like ADHD becoming more commonly recognized now than before as well as prescriptions of anti-depressant medications for younger clients.

21

Internet treatments for depression: Adults

ICBT for depression in adults is the most studied topic in the field, with a large number of trials as well as meta-analysis including IPDMA's. It is also the condition on which factorial design trials are published, and much of the research on process and mechanisms have been done in association with ICBT depression trials (Andersson, 2024). ICBT for depression was initially developed from self-help books and CCBT (see Chapters 2 and 3), and the first studies were done in the early 2000s (Andersson, 2018). As for adolescents, programs and trials have focused on prevention, symptoms of depression and diagnosed major depression. In addition, there are programs aimed at relapse prevention of new episodes. Comparisons against face-to-face, long-term effects, cost-effectiveness and also different forms of CBT and other psychotherapy orientations have been developed and tested. In fact, only focusing on depression would be a book on its own, and therefore I will cover the evidence and programs here in a more condensed manner.

Target groups and programs

I assume many readers know the scope of the problem, with depression being one of the most common mental health diagnoses and indeed health problem in general. Depression is much more common among women than men, but men can also be depressed. While depression often comes in episodes, there are many persons with chronic depression/dysthymia. Less common are other

DOI: 10.4324/9781003453444-23

affective disorders, such as bipolar disorder for which few ICBT studies have been done (Nielssen et al., 2023). There are numerous both medical and psychological treatments for depression, of which several can be regarded as evidence-based (Cuijpers et al., 2020). It is also the diagnosis for which the effects of different psycho-therapy orientations often are equal (the so-called dodo bird effect). Moreover, ICBT for depression is also the condition for which there has been most cultural adaptions of programs, and also much imple-mentation work.

CBT for depression can include several different components, which is reflected in the ICBT literature as well. Cognitive therapy and behavioural activation are often included, but given the comorbidity between depression and other problems, transdiagnostic and tailored treatments have been developed and tested (see Chapter 23). Treatment programs vary in length but should pref-erably last at least eight weeks in our experience. Various support forms have been used in research, ranging from unguided to blended treatments with substantial therapist interaction. As with CBT in general, homework is an integral part in ICBT for depression.

The evidence

Early research was mainly focused on prevention with small effects and also problem-solving therapy. When our first controlled trial was published (Andersson et al., 2005), it was initially regarded as an outlier in an early systematic review on ICBT as the effects were surprisingly large. Subsequent research showed that guided ICBT could yield large effects, and it is now fairly established that guided ICBT can be as effective as face-to-face CBT (Kambeitz-Ilankovic et al., 2022). Several meta-analyses have been published on, for example, diagnosed major depression (Königbauer et al., 2017), showing a large effect based on 10 studies compared against control conditions ($g = 0.90$). Several IPDMAs have also been published (e.g., Karyotaki et al., 2018) and others as well using similar data sets which support the early findings that guided ICBT is more effective than unguided ICBT overall. This finding still appears to hold when it comes to depression (Moshe et al., 2021). In addition, while there are fewer studies, ICBT can be used to prevent new episodes of depression (Holländare et al., 2011).

Effectiveness studies, with sometimes large data sets, have been published, suggesting that ICBT for depression works in clinically representative settings (Etzelmueller et al., 2020).

One more recent development in the field is to run factorial design trials which can isolate effects of different treatment components. Factorial design trials are more feasible to conduct in the internet setting as larger sample sizes are possible (see Chapter 11). Watkins et al. (2023) did a large factorial design depression trial in which 767 participants were included. Participants were randomly assigned to 32 experimental conditions testing the presence or absence of seven treatment components. While large improvements overall were observed, there were no large main effects, and perhaps this was because of shared features across conditions. Overall, it appears to be fairly common in factorial design trials to see no major differences, even if we in our group did detect one surprising main effect of own choice (Andersson et al., 2023). I will comment on this study in Chapter 23.

As ICBT for depression in adults has existed for some years now, it is not surprising that it has been spread to other languages and cultures than the standard WEIRD population with Western cultural background. One example from my group is a controlled trial on ICBT for depression in the Kurdish language/dialect Sorani (Lindegaard et al., 2019), which showed a large between-group effect (Cohen's $d = 1.27$), but there are other studies as well suggesting that ICBT can be delivered in other cultural settings (see Chapter 13).

Reflections

Both researchers and clinicians might rightfully wonder if we need to do more ICBT trials on adults with depression. My response is that there is still a need to answer new research questions, for example, the topic I discussed earlier in this book on knowledge acquisition, and perhaps more importantly the dilemma that we are still not very good at treating clients with chronic depression. On the other hand, the likelihood that most treatments for mild to moderate depression are about as effective (or perhaps as ineffective for some clients) still holds. It is also worth mentioning that combination treatments with, for example, a CBT rationale and physical activity is yet not much studied (Nyström et al., 2017), and that includes combined ICBT and medication as well, even if we know that stable antidepressant medication does not seem to influence the effects of ICBT (Edmonds et al., 2020). We also need to consider the WEIRD problem and work on cultural adaption of ICBT for settings in which there is still no or very limited research and implementations (for example, South America and Africa).

22

Internet treatments for depression:
Older adults

Old age is not an obvious concept in treatment research, and as I mentioned in Chapter 19, individual differences should be considered as well as the fact that most ICBT depression studies on adults have included persons aged 60 years or older. But there are some aspects to consider when doing ICBT with older persons. First, the diagnosis of depression is much more likely to be influenced by somatic factors such as diseases and impairments (e.g., hearing loss), but also cognitive decline (e.g., vascular depression) that may be hard to differentiate if the person was high functioning from the start (for example, with a university education). On the other hand, milder forms of cognitive decline may not be a problem, and the treatment format, which allows for breaks and repetition (which is different from face-to-face therapy) and also work from home, may facilitate for the more frail older person to engage in ICBT. Second, even if most people in society are computer literate, it is more likely that older persons experience problems with technology.

Target groups and programs

To the best of my knowledge, among the first to do studies on older adults were researchers in the Netherlands, who focused on symptoms of depression and a low definition of old age (50 years). By far most research on older adults with depression has been done in Australia and by the two research clinics *This Way Up* and *MindSpot*.

DOI: 10.4324/9781003453444-24

We have done a study in Sweden as well and also translated and tested our protocol in Lithuania (both not yet published). When it comes to programs, the Australian transdiagnostic program is the most commonly tested with the strongest research support. In their five-lesson transdiagnostic program, they include elements such as psychoeducation, controlling physical symptoms (anxiety management), basic principles of cognitive therapy, behavioural activation and relapse prevention (Dear et al., 2013). But they also add extra optional lessons like sleep management, communication skills, assertiveness, problem-solving, worry and attention control, which makes the transdiagnostic treatment more tailored (see Chapter 23). Our program tailors the treatment and includes only two standard modules (introduction and relapse prevention). The rest are tailored based on symptoms: behavioural activation, acceptance, sleep disturbances, worry and anxiety, loneliness, pain, applied relaxation, the nature of emotions and a life-review module. This means that the main ICBT programs for older adults have taken a transproblematic/transdiagnostic approach, which, by definition, makes it harder to say what works for whom but also makes much sense from a clinical point of view.

The evidence

I rely here on one recent systematic review and meta-analysis which included nine studies and a total of 1272 old participants (Xiang et al., 2020). There were only three randomized controlled trials, but overall they reported a mean within-group effect size of $d = 1.27$ and a mean between-group effect size of $d = 1.18$. This is also in line with our two unpublished trials. Another way to get an impression of how well ICBT for depression works in older adults is to conduct IPDMAs. In fact, we are in the process of writing up such a study based on Swedish depression trials, and when considering adults aged 65 years or older, a sample of 115 participants are in the data set derived from 11 studies. The within-group effect for these persons on the main depression measure (Beck Depression Inventory) is $d = 1.14$, which is very similar to the meta-analytic findings and clinical findings from Australia.

Reflections

In a book like this some topics need to be mentioned more than one time, and when it comes to older adults it is important to note that the comorbid somatic symptoms can be regarded as primary and therefore nested within problems like heart disease and hearing loss. I will comment on ICBT for somatic health problems in Chapter 27, but it is a well-known fact that a majority of older persons suffer from health problems. Another topic I will return to is ICBT for informal caregivers in Chapter 24. This is important as many older adults are informal caregivers of their spouse, child or other close person.

Overall, however, I believe we can conclude that ICBT could be a treatment option for older adults with depression, in particular as older adults tend to be less often offered psychological treatment and instead are only prescribed antidepressants in spite of some issues with medication such as uncertain evidence base, increased risk of side effects and multiple other medications (Tham et al., 2016).

23

Transdiagnostic and tailored internet treatments

Given the substantial symptom overlap and preferences for different treatment components, transdiagnostic and tailored ICBT treatment approaches have been developed and tested (tailored treatments have been mentioned several times in this book). In face-to-face CBT training programs, it is common to teach case formulation/ behaviour analysis to inform treatment planning and subsequent treatment. However, manualized treatments based on diagnoses leave less room for individualization of treatment components. Transdiagnostic treatments have the underlying idea that there are commonalities in terms of processes and symptoms across disorders, and that techniques like exposure can be relevant for many conditions, as well as emotion regulation and cognitive work. Tailored and transdiagnostic approaches are very different. Basically, one size fits all (or at least many) in transdiagnostic approaches versus the notion that an individual can have a unique personalized treatment and that specific solutions are required for specific problems (like insomnia). Transdiagnostic and tailored treatments can therefore be regarded as two different ways to handle the same problem of overlapping diagnoses. As I referred to in the previous chapter, there are also programs that are best represented as mixing fixed transdiagnostic and problem-specific tailored components like the MindSpot Clinic programs. In fact, in our work the first tailoring of ICBT was implemented in a tinnitus program dating back to 2000. The tailoring consisted of modules for problems not shared by all clients, in the case of tinnitus insomnia, noise sensitivity and hearing loss (see Chapter 27). Later on we also

DOI: 10.4324/9781003453444-25

implemented aspects of tailoring in, for example, a program for eating disorders, but before that we did studies on tailored ICBT for anxiety disorders as well as depression. Now tailoring is a common way to do research on new problems, for example, when the Covid-19 pandemic occurred (Aminoff et al., 2021).

Target groups and programs

The target groups for transdiagnostic treatments are often characterized by symptoms of anxiety and depression, which usually means some diagnoses are to be excluded from trials like persons with PTSD and OCD. Transdiagnostic treatments may, however, be suitable for specific target populations, such as persons with somatic problems, and it needs to be said that internet-based mindfulness and relaxation programs also can be regarded as transdiagnostic. Tailored approaches are limited by the number of conditions and problems covered by modules used for tailoring. For example, in tailored ICBT, insomnia can be covered, which is often not the case in transdiagnostic treatments (the Australian ICBT solution is an exception). Further, tailoring does not preclude shared components, and it is perfectly possible that a tailored and manual-based approach end up very similar. For example, a person getting tailored treatment for panic disorder may get more or less the same material as in a panic program. What tailoring mainly handles is preferences and perhaps also previous experiences of CBT which could influence motivation. Preferences and previous treatment experiences can be discussed in interviews informing later module selection. But tailoring can also be done by the patient (Andersson et al., 2011), which I will return to as it is a very unique way to do psychological treatment.

When it comes to tailoring, it is also the case that with each new problem for which modules are developed (like procrastination and loneliness), it will be possible to derive modules for tailored treatments when the problem is present. To give an example of module setup, the modules from a recent depression trial can be presented (Andersson et al., 2023). These covered introduction, behavioural activation I, behavioural activation II, cognitive restructuring, acceptance, emotion regulation, anxiety and exposure, social anxiety, worry, panic, insomnia, perfectionism, stress management and closure/relapse prevention. There are several other modules that can be used, and in an ongoing trial we have included financial problems and low self-esteem. It is most likely important not to overwhelm participants with modules, and prioritization might be needed. On the other hand, having much to choose from is less of a problem if the selection process is smooth, and we do this by having descriptions of modules to inform decision making for the clients when self-tailoring.

The evidence

There are more reviews covering transdiagnostic internet treatments than tailored ones. Most of the work on tailored ICBT has been done by us in Sweden, but there are other studies from, for example, Switzerland (Berger et al., 2014) showing very similar results. One systematic review covered both treatment formats and included 19 controlled trials with a total of 2952 participants (Păsărelu et al., 2017). Five were on tailored ICBT and the rest on transdiagnostic ICBT, with a majority being conducted in Australia. Overall, large between-group effect sizes were observed for measures of anxiety $g = 0.82$ and depression $g = 0.79$, with no difference between formats for those two outcomes. It should be reiterated that at least the Australian version of transdiagnostic ICBT includes self-tailoring options which was not considered in the review. Since the publication of the review, several more studies have been published including many from Canada, and there are now at least 17 trials on transdiagnostic ICBT and 12 on tailored ICBT plus several unpublished trials. An interesting new finding in controlled trials is the observation that self-tailoring seems to work, both for depression (Andersson et al., 2023) and for generalized anxiety disorder (Dahlin et al., 2022). It is most likely the case that both transdiagnostic and tailored ICBT works more or less as well for many common mental health problems. It is still uncertain regarding more specific problems, but future research might answer that, and the possibility to combine tailoring and standard components is attractive for clients, as we experienced in an eating disorder trial (Strandskov et al., 2017).

Reflections

I do believe that ICBT can help bring the field of CBT forward as we now can get evidence-based answers to important questions not previously tested in research. Tailoring makes much sense for clinicians, but there are several questions left to answer and also possible future development using AI both for treatment selection and for treatment development of tailored ICBT. Transdiagnostic ICBT also holds promise as a way to get answers on change mechanisms as fixed treatment sequences are useful in order to investigate change processes.

24

Problem-focused internet treatments I

Many studies and meta-analyses have been done on the major common diagnoses and symptoms, including somatic problems covered later on in this book. In the following two chapters I will provide examples of problem-focused ICBT programs. There are now several programs focused on topics like loneliness and procrastination. It is of course the case that persons who have problems with, say, perfectionism also are likely to suffer from symptoms like anxiety and low mood, but the notion behind the problem-focused treatments is the observation that clients may perceive problems like poor self-esteem as their main problem for which they seek help. This line of research illustrates the potential of ICBT to innovate CBT in general, as the research evaluation can be done much faster than in regular face-to-face research.

In contrast to the common psychiatric disorders, it is not always known how common clinically relevant psychological problems are. We do know that loneliness is common, but one hurdle is the use of different definitions of problems like perfectionism and relationship problems. Popular press often publish articles on these psychological problems, not seldom with alarming numbers (like 30% of the population being perfectionists). For our purpose here it is sufficient to know that it is well worth the time and effort to develop problem-focused interventions, and it is also very much in line with how clinicians work. As a therapist told me long ago, "I work with my patients' problems, not their diagnoses".

Problem-focused treatments are also interesting from a theoretical point of view when we wonder about underlying mechanisms

DOI: 10.4324/9781003453444-26

behind problems and disorders. It is, for example, often observed that perfectionism is involved in eating disorders, and loneliness is, in my experience, common among persons with social anxiety or depression, just to give a few examples. When it comes to treatment contents, it is fairly common in my group that we recycle treatment material but adapt modules for the specific problem. For example, behaviour activation in the treatment of loneliness. However, there are also more unique components, for example, in couples therapy. Moreover, transdiagnostic components and treatments may also be useful like problem-solving therapy and more bodily oriented components like applied relaxation. In fact, tailored treatments covered in the previous chapter can also be a feasible approach when the problem is less well known (for example, reactions during the Covid-19 pandemic).

It will not be possible to cover the whole literature, and I will most likely miss some problems or ongoing research that is not yet published. In this first problem-focused chapter I will review programs and studies on perfectionism, procrastination, loneliness, self-criticism, poor self-esteem, grief, couples therapy, parent training, informal caregivers, infertility distress, Covid-19 and climate anxiety.

Target groups and programs

In this section I will refer to reviews if possible, but otherwise just give references for the reader to look further as the field moves on very rapidly. Sometimes there is a long line of research, but for several problems there are just a few trials or even just one. Overall, the approach of developing and testing problem-focused ICBT has worked well, and even replications across countries have been done.

Perfectionism has been studied in some studies, with the first one dating back in 2012, and overall moderate to large between-group effects have often been observed when compared against no-treatment control (Iliakis & Masland, 2023). There are fewer trials on *procrastination* and no meta-analysis, but the trials that exist suggest large effects and similar effects as in face-to-face treatment (Rozental et al., 2018). *Loneliness* has attracted much interest, and not the least during the pandemic and also with a focus on older adults. I could not locate a broader meta-analysis on adults, but the trials that exist suggest that ICBT is a feasible treatment option for adults who experience significant loneliness (Käll et al., 2021). A related topic is the experience of *moving to a new town*, and a recent controlled trial conducted in Poland showed that ICBT can be helpful for that problem as well (Maj et al., 2024). Problems with *self-criticism* can often be seen when working with depressed clients but is significant enough to merit a focused treatment. Krieger et al. (2019) developed and tested such a program and found medium to large effects against the control group. Somewhat related is the problem of *low self-esteem* we decided to focus on when running studies on adolescents with depression and anxiety. The program and trial we then developed and tested showed that self-esteem could be improved (Berg et al., 2022).

Grief and also grief after *bereavement* can be related to both PTSD and depression, and there have been some ICBT studies on this topic, as summarized in a systematic review (Zuelke et al., 2021). Effects seem to be moderate, but it can also be the case that different treatment modalities explain this somewhat smaller effect. Internet-based *couples therapy* has been tested, and in a scoping review on dyadic internet interventions the field was covered, but there were also gaps in the literature (Shaffer et al., 2020). One study in this field should be mentioned as it tested effects for distressed low-income couples (Doss et al., 2020), which is an important contribution given the WEIRD problem in research. While moderate effects on relationship functioning were found, the effects were overall small. Another topic is *parent training for children with conduct problems*, and indeed there are programs and controlled trials on that and related topics as well (McAloon & de la Poer Beresford, 2023). Most studies in the review reported statistically significant effects.

The list of problem and areas for which there are programs continues, and I will give a few more examples. In addition to the dyadic treatments and parent training programs, we can add recent research on support for *informal adult caregivers* (Biliunaite et al., 2021). A surprisingly large proportion of adults are informal caregivers (about 10% in Sweden), and for them getting psychological support from a distance can be preferred when, for example, caring for a partner with dementia. The controlled trial conducted in Lithuania showed promising results with reduced caregiver burden. Another problem for which there are just a few studies is distress experienced in association with *infertility* and assisted reproductive technology. I mention here an interesting study conducted in Iran in which ICBT was compared against face-to-face treatment with equal effects (Shafierizi et al., 2023), in line with our meta-analysis (Hedman-Lagerlöf et al., 2023).

The *Covid-19 pandemic* was, as I mentioned early in this book, described as a "Black Swan" for internet interventions (Wind et al., 2020), and indeed online treatments including video therapy went from being an alternative to a strongly recommended way to deliver CBT. We began doing tailored ICBT already during the first summer after the onset of the pandemic (Aminoff et al., 2021), and also did a trial during the second wave in the spring of 2022 (Aminoff et al., 2023). There were other trials done as well. Overall, results showed that symptoms of anxiety and depression were reduced (Komariah et al., 2022). On a related note, fatigue is a common symptom following Covid infection, and there are studies on ICBT for chronic fatigue showing reliable effects (e.g., Janse et al., 2018).

Another example of a problem-focused ICBT program and study is, as far as I know, unique. We focused on *psychological distress associated with climate change*, which is often referred to in the literature as climate anxiety. We broadened the scope to other psychological reactions as well, as we believe symptoms of depression and hopelessness are important in the target group. The pilot-RCT showed promising results with moderate to large between-group effects compared to a waitlist group on measures of depression and anxiety (Lindhe et al., 2023). See Figure 24.1 for a screenshot from the Climatecope program.

Figure 24.1 Screenshot from the Climatecope program

Reflections

This chapter covered a very expansive field, and the list of possible problems for which there are no evidence-based treatments is long in spite of the many examples I provided. As I mentioned it could be argued that we do not need more controlled trials on ICBT, but I believe there is more to learn, and research studies can tell us where to go next. In particular, the problem-focused programs can be contrasted against the more diagnosis-focused and indeed transdiagnostic approaches. As we can be rather certain that the ICBT treatment format can work, it is more question of how suitable our treatment content is, which is important not only for ICBT but for the whole field of psychotherapy as well.

25

Problem-focused internet treatments II

In this chapter I cover some additional problem-focused treatments. Some diagnoses like substance use disorders are usually regarded as more severe than most of the problems I reviewed in the previous chapter. Thus I will cover here anger management, interpersonal violence, self-injury, pathological gambling and substance use disorders. The implementation of problem-focused ICBT varies a lot, but programs for pathological gambling and substance abuse disorders are implemented in some places like here in Sweden.

Target groups and programs

When it comes to *interpersonal violence, victims of violence* and *anger management*, there has been much research, with most being focused on prevention. I focus here on ICBT programs. A few promising controlled trials show that maladaptive anger can be treated (Bjureberg, Ojala, Berg, et al., 2023), mild interpersonal conflicts/violence reduced (Hesser et al., 2017), victims of interpersonal violence with residual problems be helped (Andersson et al., 2021) as well as victims of bullying (Thorisdottir & Asmundson, 2022). Some research has also been done on *non-suicidal self-injury* (Bjureberg, Ojala, Hesser, et al., 2023). A somewhat related problem is the unique research recently done to help *users of online child sexual abuse material* reduce their consumption of such material. In a controlled trial conducted via the Darknet, reductions were found, but with small effects (Lätth et al., 2022). This study and the project is very special. For a start it was very important for the participants not to be identified, but at the same time ethics and an obligation to report ongoing abuse was also part of the protocol. All participants were interviewed, and it was clear from the start that the study concerned use of online sexual abuse material, but that is of course indirectly related to actual abuse of children, and an industry that is maintained by consumers of such material. On the other hand, the purpose of the research was to help people reduce or preferably totally stop using such material. From a technical point of view, delivering the intervention via Darknet was a challenge. The program contained eight modules covering a) Introduction to CBT. Functional analyses and treatment goals; b) Exploring life balance based on the excessive and deficient behaviours model; c) Psychoeducation about uncontrolled sexuality. The function of sexual behaviours and maintenance factors; d) Exploring ambivalence about changing sexual behaviour(s), in order to increase motivation; e) Mindfulness and skills training. Risk situations; increased awareness and alternative behaviours; f) Identifying core values and related goals. Improving goal setting and stress management skills to work towards goals; g) Behavioural experiments to start striving towards identified goals and identify specific factors related to increased risk. Psychoeducation about children's inability to consent to sex; h) Summary. Creating a maintenance program to continue managing risk situations and working towards goals based on core values. This program is an example of a problem-focused program for which new material had to be developed.

Much research has been done on pathological gambling/gaming disorders. A fairly recent systematic review by Sagoe et al. (2021) reported effects on general gambling symptoms ($g = 0.73$), gambling frequency ($g = 0.29$) and amount of money lost gambling ($g = 0.19$), based on 13 studies. In Sweden ICBT for gambling problems is implemented in Stockholm. There is much more I could cover here, including work I have been involved in as well, but for the present overview we can just conclude that this is an active and important field. The same can be said about substance use disorders, for which much ICBT work has been done, mainly on alcohol but also for other addictions. A comprehensive scoping review by Johansson et al. (2024) of a very large literature highlighted unclear descriptions, weak support for some intervention, limited research on some targets groups and few economic assessments. However, on a more positive note, there is great potential in doing research for these problems and some good examples, even if effects overall tend to be small compared to what we usually see in ICBT trials. Important work is also done on different forms of substance use, for example, cannabis use (Boumparis et al., 2019), even if, again, effects tend to be much smaller than we see in anxiety and depression trials.

Reflections

This chapter included problems that are more challenging to treat than some other problems in the previous chapter (for example, procrastination). For example, substance use disorders, and perhaps more challenging use of illegal substances, can be viewed as examples of problems where stigma and unwillingness to be identified plays a major role. The way we do studies usually means being identified, and the role of anonymous treatments has, to the best of my knowledge, not been studied much on ICBT research.

26

Eating disorders, insomnia, stress, sexual health and neurological conditions

Target groups and programs

Starting off with *eating disorders*, there is a fairly large ICBT literature focusing on programs for bulimia, binge eating disorder and eating disorders not otherwise specified. Cases of anorexia nervosa have usually not been included in most of this work, with the exception of a few relapse prevention studies (e.g., Jacobi et al., 2023). A majority of the work has been based on CBT protocols, but there are also influences from ACT (Strandskov et al., 2017). While there are not numerous studies, there are findings supporting the effects of guided ICBT and also internet-delivered prevention programs (Hamid, 2024). When it comes to average effects, prevention programs showed a moderate effect (e.g., SMD = 0.46), whereas intervention studies had, on average, larger effects (e.g., SMD = 0.70). To the best of my knowledge, implementation of ICBT for eating disorders also exists in few places in the world.

Obesity and overweight are major challenges for society and have also been studied for many years in the ICBT literature (with the common dilemma of different terminologies being present as several studies and review refer to web-based digital interventions). A fairly recent systematic review concluded that internet interventions can lead to short-term weight loss, but, as is the case with face-to-face treatments, long-term effects are more disappointing (Beleigoli et al., 2019). Interestingly, and in one way a sensible way to describe results, the metric described was actual weight loss in kg. The authors reported that digital inventions were

DOI: 10.4324/9781003453444-28

more effective than control conditions in terms of average weight loss (on average 2.13 kg), but not in the long run (mean difference of 0.17 kg).

One of the earliest problems we focused on in my group was *insomnia*. This is a very common problem in society, and also often comorbid with both mental and somatic health problems. We were most likely first in the world to do ICBT for insomnia, and published our findings a few years later (Ström et al., 2004). After that several ICBT programs were developed and tested, usually incorporating standard components found to be useful for insomnia (e.g., stimulus control, sleep restriction, sleep hygiene, etc.). One recent systematic review and network meta-analysis summarized the findings that both guided and unguided ICBT can be effective (Simon et al., 2023). Both guided ICBT (SMD = 0.71) and unguided (SMD = 0.78) yielded good effects with the somewhat surprising lack of differences between guided and unguided ICBT. In fact, this could be an example of a condition for which unguided ICBT is suitable without any loss of effect. ICBT for insomnia is implemented in several clinical settings.

Stress is also a common problem in society and associated with a range of negative consequences including reduced work capacity. We were early with this problem and published our first controlled trial more the 20 years back (Zetterqvist et al., 2003). Svärdman et al. (2022) published a meta-analysis of 14 ICBT studies and reported a large average treatment effect (Cohen's d = 0.78). Further, ICBT for stress has been implemented in, for example, Sweden.

Sexual problems can be embarrassing, and therefore ICBT can be an attractive treatment alternative. Indeed, when we ran a study on *erectile dysfunction*, the recruitment of participants was very rapid, which suggests there is a great need for treatment. There are different sexual health problems in addition to erectile dysfunction, such as vulvodynia. Overall sexual problems can be described as disorders of sexual desire/interest, arousal, orgasm and sexual pain. I found one systematic review and meta-analysis on this topic, and results were promising, but effects appeared to be small to moderate when compared against control conditions (Zarski et al., 2022).

Interestingly, they noted gender differences as results regarding female sexual functioning ($g=0.59$) and satisfaction ($g=0.90$) appeared to be larger than for male sexual functioning ($g=0.18$). There were no significant effects found for male sexual satisfaction as results were heterogeneous.

I mention here briefly neurological and neuropsychiatric conditions. Programs and trials have been published on epilepsy, Parkinson's disease, spinal cord injury, multiple sclerosis, high-functioning autism spectrum disorder and ADHD, just to give a few examples. This work is less spread and there are fewer studies, but it is an interesting development with some promising results (e.g., Gandy et al., 2020; Gold et al., 2023). Indeed, for ADHD I found one meta-analysis based on six controlled trials showing an effect of SMD = 0.79 (Shou et al., 2022).

Reflections

Several of the conditions covered in this chapter are both very common and also mostly suitable for ICBT. As often is the case, the results of ICBT mirrors the effects of face-to-face CBT, and therefore it is not surprising that results regarding, for example, obesity are not that great, whereas for insomnia and stress, effects tend to be larger. There is much research activity overall, but, as noted, more needs to be done regarding neurological and neuropsychiatric conditions, in order to know if they lend themselves to ICBT.

Somatic disorders

I began my ICBT research with a study on headache initiated by two students in 1998 (Ström et al., 2000). The research on ICBT for somatic disorders and conditions is almost as extensive as the work on mental health problems and could merit a separate volume. My research group has benefitted from working with both psychiatric and somatic health problems (and also problem-specific programs), as it is often the same person who may suffer from depression AND, for example, chronic pain. Unfortunately, the comorbidity between somatic and mental health problems is not always recognized in the CBT literature, but I will do my best here to cover the main conditions in the field. In fact, this includes several major health problems.

Problems and programs

We started early with *chronic pain*, with the first trial published 20 years back (Buhrman et al., 2004). Since then many programs and trials have been conducted with several different approaches, including mainly CBT and ACT components but also applied relaxation and mindfulness techniques. One of the more recent systematic reviews included as many as 36 studies (Gandy et al., 2022), but, in line with the face-to-face literature on chronic pain, effects are not as great as for many other problems (for example, Hedges' $g = 0.28$ on measures of pain interference/disability). It is important to note that there are exceptions, with a few programs and trials

DOI: 10.4324/9781003453444-29

showing larger effects but also findings suggesting that long-term effects are limited. ICBT for chronic pain has been implemented in some places, including Australia and Sweden. There are also studies on *headache*, which followed our first controlled trial (Ström et al., 2000), and even earlier trials from Germany. There are also studies on pain-related problems such as *whiplash, rheumatoid arthritis, spinal cord injury, fibromyalgia* (Mehta et al., 2019) and studies on concurrent problems like insomnia and chronic pain. A somewhat related condition is *irritable bowel syndrome* for which there are controlled trials showing good results (Kim et al., 2022).

Tinnitus is defined as ringing or buzzing in the ear(s) with no external origin. It is a very common condition, with a 15% prevalence in adults, and more severe tinnitus being present in as many as 3% of the adult population. It is the condition I have worked with as a clinician for 30 years, and I see tinnitus patients at the hospital every week. Given this it was rather expected that tinnitus became the second topic to focus on when we started running ICBT studies (Andersson et al., 2002). Since then our initial results have been replicated several times, and most recently in Lithuania and earlier in Germany, United Kingdom and United States. We have also developed and tested an ACT version of our tinnitus treatment. Based on nine controlled trials, Beukes et al. (2019) reported a moderate effect size against passive control conditions. Overall, effects on tinnitus distress have been moderate to large, and long-term effects have been reported. There are a few programs and trials on internet interventions for hearing loss and dizziness/vestibular difficulties, but not enough for a meta-analytic summary.

Different forms of *cancer* and problems related to cancer are both common and also the topic of much psychosocial research. A significant proportion of the programs and research can be categorized as ICBT, but not all. It is a scattered literature, but with some promising findings when it comes to symptoms of depression and anxiety (Zhang et al., 2024). An impression is that ICBT can be useful for handling the psychological consequences for cancer survivors, but also that most research has been done on women and breast cancer and, to a lesser extent, men with, for example, prostate cancer.

As with cancer, *heart failure and cardiovascular diseases* are common, and many people survive but their quality of life is negatively affected. I have a close collaboration with nurses who have adapted a depression program for heart failure and symptoms of depression (Johansson et al., 2019). As with cancer there are programs and studies that cannot be described as ICBT, and with regards to ICBT, findings have been mixed. There are, for example, trials with poor adherence and minor effects. This is a field in which more research is needed.

Sometimes associated with cardiovascular disease is the common problem *diabetes*. There are ICBT studies sometimes showing large effects (Mehta et al., 2019). But there are not many studies yet, in spite of the large number of persons who have both diabetes and psychological distress (Tavares Franquez et al., 2023).

Reflections

Many programs and trials have been done on somatic disorders and related health conditions. Most likely guided ICBT can help to reduce symptoms like anxiety and depression (White et al., 2022) but is less effective in reducing more symptom-specific problems and functional impairments, even if there are exceptions. As I write this book I am amazed by the extreme productivity and also the speed of actually finalizing and publishing trials. This is unique and has never been seen before in the history of psychotherapy and CBT. Perhaps even in medicine in general, as, for example, trials on medications can take a long time to conduct. Indeed, in particular, for the somatic health problems, there are new ICBT programs and applications which arguably broaden the scope of CBT in general. I could not cover everything in this chapter. For example, studies on women's health with problems like fear of childbirth and trauma following childbirth. Added to that is the problem of postpartum depression and also depression and anxiety during pregnancy. I conclude with the observation that the scope for ICBT for persons with somatic health problems is growing as more patients with, for example, cancer and cardiovascular disease now survive but can still experience psychological distress for many years after being treated for their medical condition.

28

Other treatment orientations

I will comment here on some other treatment orientations such as physical activity, psychodynamic psychotherapy and interpersonal psychotherapy. Moreover, I will also cover acceptance and commitment therapy, mindfulness and motivational interviewing, which could be regarded as part of or versions of CBT.

Other therapeutic orientations and their effects

Given the speed of development of internet interventions programs and relative ease of running trials, it is not surprising that other forms of psychological treatments than CBT have been developed and tested. There are fewer programs and studies on these other treatment orientations, but it is still an important literature to consider, as we in the future are likely to borrow from each other and perhaps even integrate treatment techniques from different approaches (as has been done with, for example, mindfulness).

If I start with the programs close to CBT, there have been several internet-delivered programs and studies on *mindfulness*. Sometimes the mindfulness techniques are part of a comprehensive CBT protocol, for example, in our tailored ICBT programs, but there are also programs and studies in which mindfulness is the main or even only method. In fact, this literature is now divided into different target problems, with trials and systematic reviews being published. In my group we did our first "pure" mindfulness trial more than 10 years ago, but other researchers had already started by then. In one systematic review on internet-delivered mindfulness for mental health problems, moderate effects were noted (Sevilla-Llewellyn-Jones et al., 2018), but there have been several studies since that trial showing statistically significant improvements.

Another treatment orientation – *acceptance and commitment therapy* (ACT) – is, in my opinion, a form of CBT. It has, however, somewhat different theoretical assumptions than standard CBT and important considerations of values, willingness and committed action without sacrificing important CBT methods like exposure. As with mindfulness, we have incorporated ACT components in our tailored programs but also tested ACT separately for different conditions like tinnitus, chronic pain and depression. In one recent review of the internet-based ACT literature, Han and Kim (2022) covered several trials and overall found small to moderate effects when passive control conditions were used, and minor or no effects when active controls were analysed. This is an example of how meta-analyses run the risk of conflating different control groups and misrepresent the literature if results are combined, as an active control condition not seldom is a psychological treatment (and not placebo or just attention control), for which no differences are expected.

When it comes to *motivational interviewing* as a therapeutic approach, there are examples of ICBT trials in which it has been included before ICBT (Soucy et al., 2021), and is often present in the literature on substance use disorders. Findings are mixed but appear to boost engagement.

Physical activity as an internet intervention can be framed as behavioural activation, and indeed there are a trials on depression and anxiety, with online physical activity as the treatment showing moderate to large effects (Chen et al., 2024). We have done a few trials showing positive outcomes. My own view is that physical activity can be combined with ICBT, and we also have it as a module in some programs.

Psychodynamic internet treatment has mainly been studied in Sweden, with some additional studies from Germany and United Kingdom. The background for us was that we needed an active control condition in a study on GAD. As results for psychodynamic guided self-help was promising, we moved on to other conditions and target groups, and most recently adolescents with depression in a large trial showing non-inferiority against ICBT (Mechler et al., 2022). The effects of internet-based psychodynamic treatment has been summarized in a separate meta-analysis (Lindegaard et al., 2020), and our studies are also included in reviews of psychodynamic treatment in general. There are, however, very few internet-delivered programs and studies, and more will most likely be developed in the future.

Another form of psychotherapy is *interpersonal psychotherapy* (IPT). We have tested this as a comparison group in one trial on social anxiety disorder (Dagöö et al., 2014) and one on loneliness (Käll et al., 2021), and in both, IPT delivered via the internet was less effective than ICBT. There are a few more trials including one we have done on depression, but to date, it might be that IPT is less feasible to transfer to the guided self-help format.

Reflections

I believe that the internet format of running trials already has innovated psychotherapy research, and it is almost strange to note that the largest comparative trials on different psychotherapy orientations are done via the internet. This calls for an investigation of the old idea that all psychotherapies are about as effective – the so-called "dodo bird" effect. We are in the process of studying what we call the "digital dodo", and it will be interesting to know the limits of the dodo verdict, as we have seen examples of slightly inferior treatments (for example, attention bias modification and perhaps IPT). There are few programs in which the humanistic therapy tradition is spelled out. Some of the techniques and ideas, however, live on in, for example, ACT, and existential issues are definitely present in some ICBT programs and studies. Finally, we have done a few "preference" trials, in which we have allowed our participants to choose a therapy form (Johansson et al., 2013). This could be a way to bring forward the research on what works for whom as preferences are known to affect outcomes.

29

Experiences of clients and clinicians

Most research findings covered in this book have been quantitative, using controlled research designs, validated outcome measures and, after that, summarized in systematic reviews and meta-analyses. But in order to learn more about how ICBT works, we can also get information in an open-ended manner from our clients using qualitative methods. We began fairly early to do qualitative studies in association with the controlled trials, with one of the first being on depression (Bendelin et al., 2011). That study was very informative as it made us realize that there were clients in treatment who completed all the modules but still did not engage or change their lives. We now usually plan qualitative studies as part of our new programs and controlled trials, which has led to several publications. Often we use thematic analysis following open-ended telephone interviews that are transcribed and then analysed. Samples in qualitative studies are usually smaller than quantitative studies (N = 10–15), and therefore we use strategic sampling of clients with different experiences (e.g., not only the successful cases). For readers who are familiar with qualitative methods, it can be good to know that almost all studies have been "close to the data", and there are fewer studies using methods like discourse analysis (for example, by using chat interactions) or phenomenological methods like interpretative phenomenological analysis. In my opinion, qualitative research methods require suitable data, and therefore interviews are needed. There are studies using text responses to open-ended questions, and that can generate interesting findings, but short texts are less suitable for more in-depth analysis (rather, content analysis should be used).

DOI: 10.4324/9781003453444-31

Some examples

As for the controlled trials with systematic reviews, it is possible to do systematic reviews of qualitative studies. I am only aware of one. Patel et al. (2020) did a review of qualitative studies and a so-called meta-synthesis of the ICBT studies. Based on 24 studies reviewed, they identified three key themes: initial motivations and approaches to internet interventions, personalization of treatment and the value of receiving personal support. This fits in well with the findings from our qualitative studies (some of which were included in this review).

Typical of ICBT research, much has been published when we now turn to the qualitative studies on ICBT just a few years after the meta-synthesis by Patel et al. (2020). One example is a study from Lithuania in which reasons for usage discontinuation of ICBT for stress was investigated (Nomeikaite et al., 2023). They included 12 telephone interviews which were transcribed and analysed using thematic analysis. Results showed that personal aspects including life circumstances, personal characteristics and psychological responses to the program were involved as well as program-related aspects (e.g., content and support). There are also published studies on how therapists experience ICBT and also other experiences of other stakeholders.

I mention another example from my group which underlines the importance of doing qualitative research when developing new interventions (as described in Chapter 11). When we developed a new treatment for low self-esteem in adolescents, it was important to investigate also how our trial participants had experienced the intervention (Berg et al., 2023). We were also curious about what they had learned, related to the research I mentioned in Chapter 10 on ICBT as education. We conducted telephone interviews with 15 adolescents and used inductive thematic analysis for the analysis of the transcribed interviews. Four themes were identified: a) increased awareness and agency in difficult situations, b) enhanced self-image, c) unique but not alone and d) widened understanding and new perspectives. Overall, the participants were very positive, which is rather common in the qualitative studies on ICBT but also something that can appear strange for reviewers as much qualitative research in other areas focus on negative reactions. On the other hand, negative reactions are sometimes reported as we deliberately include also trial participants who have benefitted less (and even dropped out). I give here a quote from young female participant related to the first theme:

> I also in this way accept that I am the person I am today. . . .
> I let myself have feelings and I let myself have bad moments
> instead of questioning this, I accept that I am not perfect, my
> mood is not perfect and I have to let myself be disappointed
> or angry or sad. As much as I let myself be happy and excited.

Reflections

I strongly believe qualitative and quantitative research methods complement each other, even if the assumptions and methods can be markedly different. In fact, for each new program, controlled trial and target population, it would be good to have at least one qualitative study, and it works both ways. Quantitative studies can generate ideas for qualitative research (as in the knowledge acquisition example), but qualitative studies can also help us understand our quantitative results. For example, when we did qualitative study on dropouts, important results were obtained that helped us improve our treatment program and study process, for example that lack of time and stress were reasons behind dropout (Johansson et al., 2015). Combined research methods (mixed) could also be considered, and even if they are few I expect more to come when describing, for example, treatment development using both quantitative and qualitative methods in the same study. Finally, there is a need for a new meta-synthesis of the qualitative literature as the extensive publishing in our field makes systematic reviews outdated quickly.

30

Future directions and concluding remarks

By now readers may feel overwhelmed, as there is so much done already, and ICBT seems to be very well established. There are of course negative studies, and we have also published "failed" trials (e.g., Lindh-Åstrand et al., 2015), which I believe is crucial as we learn from these and can avoid repeating mistakes. But the vast amount of studies and strong research support for several conditions can also lead to despair as there are so many programs that never reach the clinic and only end up in a publication. I have been involved in some programs that have been implemented, but many more that have not. In this final chapter I will give an overview summary of what I believe can be said about ICBT and then move on to suggest some possible future research targets.

What can be said about effects?

I think it is time now to make an attempt to summarize what most likely is the overall results of ICBT, and perhaps for psychological treatments in general as readers by now have seen that guided ICBT is as effective as face-to-face CBT, at least for the conditions tested.

I have mentioned individual patient data meta-analyses (IPDMAs) a few times in this book. We collected as much data we could from our Swedish studies and focused on response and remission rates for conditions like anxiety, depression and somatic disorders (Andersson, Carlbring, & Rozental, 2019). Based on a total of 29 studies and 2,866 patients, the criteria of reliable change index

DOI: 10.4324/9781003453444-32

(RCI z = 1.96 or more) showed that 65.6% of the patients receiving treatment were classified as achieving recovery. Adding the requirement of substantial improvement showed that 35.0% were classified as reaching remission. We used the same data set and focused on non-response (Rozental et al., 2019). Of the treated participants (n = 2118), 26.8% could be classified as non-responders defined as having less than a reliable improvement (RCI of z < 1.96). Before those two reports and as part of a PhD project, we focused on deterioration (Rozental et al., 2017). In that IPMDA we found that 5.8% in the treatment conditions reported deterioration, also using RCI as criteria. This leads me to tentatively conclude that following ICBT across conditions **35.0%** reach remission, an additional **31%** recovery (a total of **66%** improving), **27%** show a non-response and, finally, a small number of **6%** deterioration. This is not a bad result and is perhaps more easy to communicate to laypersons than our usual effect sizes and statistical significance.

I have not devoted much space in this book to the process and prediction studies. There are several studies, but very inconsistent and scattered. Luckily, the review by Haller et al. (2023) is helpful here as they summarized this large literature. I mentioned their review earlier when commenting on the role of the alliance. Apart from the fairly robust albeit small association between alliance and outcome, prediction studies do not tell us much. In fact, following collection of 60 studies and analyses of 88 predictors or moderators including some standard variables like gender, results were rather meagre. But better adherence and treatment credibility were associated with outcome in addition to the alliance, and the common finding that high baseline scores predict more improvement as well. They concluded that all other predictors/moderators were inconclusive or lacked data. For me this is not surprising as the typical intervention study has inclusion and exclusion criteria, which means the predictors of outcome are removed from the study. In real-life clinics the situation is somewhat better even if there are limits there as well and biases such as referral patterns. It would be easy to design a study with strong predictors of outcome, even if it would be ethically questionable. For example, reading skills are likely to be detrimental for text-based ICBT and low IQ as well, just to give two examples.

Are there any other limitations?

As with any treatment format, there are both pros and cons. I have mentioned several limitations related to the research done, and also the fact that exclusion criteria in studies might disguise limitations. I also mentioned the WEIRD problem present in much research. In clinical practice we have always been very clear about ICBT being a complement and sometimes replacement for face-to-face services, but that we cannot really say what works for whom. In fact, it is often the case that a person suitable for face-to-face CBT often can do guided ICBT as well. But there are exceptions. In the previous paragraph I mentioned problems with reading skills and low IQ. Some clinicians would perhaps argue that more severe clients would not be suitable for guided ICBT. However, there is not much empirical support for this claim, apart from the additional caveat that some clients are not ready or suitable for any psychological treatment. This includes risk management I commented on earlier in this book and sometimes a need to refer to specialist care (e.g., a psychiatrist). I have mentioned blended treatments several times in this book, and they can be a way to handle, for example, perceived risks and when face-to-face interactions are needed. As commented on in the book, much less work has been done on psychosis and diagnoses like borderline personality disorder. But this does not necessarily mean ICBT cannot be used for these groups, at least as a complement. It is only that the research needs to be done first (for example, work already done on bipolar disorder).

Possible future research

There are many potential ways to move this field forward, in particular in light of the many controlled trials already made. As I have implied, we might have focused too much on controlled trials, but on the other hand they are very informative, and experimental control is usually better than observational studies. I will give some examples of possible future research and practice of ICBT.

I start with *settings and populations*. While ICBT stands out in relation to usual psychotherapy research when it comes to international studies and non-Western settings, there are many countries and even continents in which very little work has been done, with South America being one example. The concept of "local evidence" should be considered, at least when there are major cultural differences and attitudes towards, for example, mental health. But this also relates to populations within countries as most research has been done on the WEIRD population, in particular when it comes to educational background. We also need to facilitate global dissemination and the concept of global mental health, which was commented on early in our field (Munoz, 2010), but still is held back by regulations and unclear rules even within Europe.

Settings and procedures are probably more important than we realize when it comes to securing treatment outcomes, and I mentioned some aspects in Chapter 15. Several ideas could be tested in research, for example, the importance of waiting times between registration and treatment, the time of the year when the treatment is delivered, the reputation of the hospital, company or university where the treatment is provided and several other aspects that we suspect might influence outcome. There are also other settings that have not been mentioned, for example, providing ICBT when waiting for another treatment (with research in transplantation patients being in progress) and also ICBT as aftercare, with early work done in Germany.

My second topic for the future relates *to treatment development*. In particular, I am optimistic about the transdiagnostic and problem-focused treatments. When it comes to the latter, there are many problems in life that could be helped with a guided ICBT that have not yet been focused on. Sometimes it can be just minor adaptions of existing programs, but, for example, providing ICBT for informal caregivers was a new challenge with not much previous intervention research to rely on. Further, and perhaps rather a question of populations, there are many different groups in society related to professions (like medical staff), and also other roles like in sports and in relation to sexual minorities that could motivate adaptions. My examples have already been studied and are underway in ICBT research. I must again admit that in spite of numerous examples, I have not covered everything. There is much less done on more severe mental health problems like schizophrenia and bipolar disorder, but this might change in the future with the important consideration that treatments for conditions like these need to be multidisciplinary with combined treatments. On the other side of the spectrum, we will most likely see development and tests of short single-session treatments, which are not suitable for most clinical conditions but very well can serve as prevention. A final example of future programs and applications is treatment for persons with financial problems. This has largely been neglected, but new research is on its way (Richardson et al., 2022). A different aspect is the probable use of AI and tools like ChatGPT to develop intervention and perhaps also support (Carlbring et al., 2023).

My third topic for the future concerns variables to be measured in research (commented on in Chapter 12). Much has been done with regards to self-report, but other ways to collect data on behaviour could be explored with the help of smartphones (Mohr et al., 2017) and perhaps even used as outcomes in trials. To date, very few have focused on learning and the educational aspects of ICBT, and that is a topic that needs more research. Moreover, while we earlier did some research using cognitive measures as outcomes (like future directed thinking), there is not much done there as well. In fact, ICBT could benefit more from cognitive science. While there has been some research on the role of genetics and also brain imaging studies, it is most likely not the most cost-effective way to bring ICBT forward even if the treatment format lends itself easily to such research. Overall, biological markers (for example, hormones) are both important and interesting, but there is yet not much research done related to ICBT, and findings are not very strong or conclusive.

I would, however, recommend researchers to consider studying not only self-reported outcomes, but I am aware of the costs.

My final topic is the use of *different analytic tools* in ICBT research. Not only do we need to keep track of the statistical tools and how to handle, for example, trajectories of change and missing data, but we also face a plethora of methods and tools related to AI and machine learning. Possibly the large data sets from ICBT clinics can be useful to make us better at predicting outcomes with the help of AI. But we might also benefit from returning to our past with case studies of treated ICBT cases. There is a huge gap in the literature here, with almost no case studies reported.

Concluding remarks

Clinicians and researchers in CBT need to know about the massive progress done in ICBT research and practice. It is also a landmark that internet approaches to psychotherapy were included in the latest edition of the *Bergin and Garfield's Handbook of Psychotherapy and Behavior Change* (Andersson & Berger, 2021). While we still will need to see some of our clients face-to-face, we should consider blending services to serve our clients better. As the treatment versus demand gap is huge when it comes to not only mental health but also psychological effects of somatic disorders and other problems, we should make an effort to disseminate ICBT to a wider group of people in the world.

References

Abbott, J. M., Kaldo, V., Klein, B., Austin, D., Hamilton, C., Piterman, L., & Andersson, G. (2009). A cluster randomised controlled trial of an internet-based intervention program for tinnitus distress in an industrial setting. *Cognitive Behaviour Therapy*, *38*, 162–173.

Ajzen, I. (1991). The theory of planned behavior. *Organizational Behavior and Human Decision Processes*, *50*, 179–211.

American Psychiatric Association. (2013). *Diagnostic and statistical manual of mental disorders. DSM-5*. American Psychiatric Press.

Aminoff, V., Bobeck, J., Hjort, S., Sörliden, E., Ludvigsson, M., Berg, M., & Andersson, G. (2023). Tailored internet-based psychological treatment for psychological problems associated with the COVID-19 pandemic: A randomized controlled trial. *Internet Interventions*, *34*, 100662.

Aminoff, V., Sellén, M., Sörliden, E., Ludvigsson, M., Berg, M., & Andersson, G. (2021). Internet-based cognitive behavioral therapy for psychological distress associated with the COVID-19 pandemic: A pilot randomized controlled trial. *Frontiers in Psychology*, *12*, 684540.

Andersson, G. (2015). *The internet and CBT: A clinical guide*. CRC Press.

Andersson, G. (2018). Internet interventions: Past, present and future. *Internet Interventions*, *12*, 181–188.

Andersson, G. (2024). The latest developments with internet-based psychological treatments for depression. *Expert Review of Neurotherapeutics*, *24*, 171–176.

Andersson, G., & Berger, T. (2021). Internet approaches to psychotherapy: Empirical findings and future directions. In M. Barkham, W. Lutz, & L. G. Castonguay (Eds.), *Bergin and Garfield's handbook of psychotherapy and behavior change* (50th anniversary ed., pp. 749–772). Wiley.

Andersson, G., Bergström, J., Holländare, F., Carlbring, P., Kaldo, V., & Ekselius, L. (2005). Internet-based self-help for depression: A randomised controlled trial. *British Journal of Psychiatry, 187,* 456–461.

Andersson, G., Carlbring, P., Berger, T., Almlöv, J., & Cuijpers, P. (2009). What makes Internet therapy work? *Cognitive Behaviour Therapy, 38,* 55–60.

Andersson, G., Carlbring, P., Furmark, T., & on behalf of the SOFIE Research Group. (2012). Therapist experience and knowledge acquisition in internet-delivered CBT for social anxiety disorder: A randomized controlled trial. *PLoS One, 7,* e37411.

Andersson, G., Carlbring, P., & Rozental, A. (2019). Response and remission rates in internet-based cognitive behavior therapy: An individual patient data meta-analysis. *Frontiers in Psychiatry, 10,* 749.

Andersson, G., Carlbring, P., Titov, N., & Lindefors, N. (2019). Internet interventions for adults with anxiety and mood disorders: A narrative umbrella review of recent meta-analyses. *Canadian Journal of Psychiatry, 64,* 465–470.

Andersson, G., & Cuijpers, P. (2009). Internet-based and other computerized psychological treatments for adult depression: A meta-analysis. *Cognitive Behaviour Therapy, 38,* 196–205.

Andersson, G., Estling, F., Jakobsson, E., Cuijpers, P., & Carlbring, P. (2011). Can the patient decide which modules to endorse? An open trial of tailored Internet treatment of anxiety disorders. *Cognitive Behaviour Therapy, 40,* 57–64.

Andersson, G., Käll, A., Juhlin, S., Wahlström, C., de Fine Licht, E., Färdeman, S., Franck, A., Tholcke, K., Nachtweij, K., Fransson, E., Vernmark, K., Ludvigsson, M., & Berg, M. (2023). Free choice of treatment content, support on demand and supervision in internet-delivered CBT for adults with depression: A randomized factorial design trial. *Behaviour Research and Therapy, 162,* 104265.

Andersson, G., Olsson, E., Ringsgård, E., Sandgren, T., Viklund, I., Andersson, C., Hesselman, Y., Johansson, R., Bergman Nordgren, L., & Bohman, B. (2021). Individually tailored internet-delivered cognitive-behavioral therapy for survivors of intimate partner violence: A randomized controlled pilot trial. *Internet Interventions*, *26*, 100453.

Andersson, G., Rozental, A., Shafran, R., & Carlbring, P. (2018). Long-term effects of internet-supported cognitive behavior therapy. *Expert Review of Neurotherapeutics*, *18*, 21–28.

Andersson, G., Sarkohi, A., Karlsson, J., Bjärehed, J., & Hesser, H. (2013). Effects of two forms of internet-delivered cognitive behaviour therapy on future thinking. *Cognitive Therapy and Research*, *37*, 29–34.

Andersson, G., Strömgren, T., Ström, L., & Lyttkens, L. (2002). Randomised controlled trial of Internet based cognitive behavior therapy for distress associated with tinnitus. *Psychosomatic Medicine*, *64*, 810–816.

Andersson, G., Waara, J., Jonsson, U., Malmaeus, F., Carlbring, P., & Öst, L.-G. (2009). Internet-based self-help vs. one-session exposure in the treatment of spider phobia: A randomized controlled trial. *Cognitive Behaviour Therapy*, *38*, 114–120.

Atzor, M.-C., Andersson, G., von Lersner, U., & Weise, C. (2024). Effectiveness of internet-based training on psychotherapists' transcultural competence: A randomized controlled trial. *Journal of Cross-Cultural Psychology*, *55*, 260–277.

Axelsson, E., & Hedman-Lagerlöf, E. (2019). Cognitive behavior therapy for health anxiety: Systematic review and meta-analysis of clinical efficacy and health economic outcomes. *Expert Review of Pharmacoeconomics & Outcomes Research*, *19*, 663–676.

Bandura, A. (1977). Self-efficacy: Toward a unifying theory of behavioral change. *Psychological Review*, *84*, 191–215.

Baumeister, H., Reichler, L., Munzinger, M., & Lin, J. (2014). The impact of guidance on internet-based mental health interventions – A systematic review. *Internet Interventions*, *1*, 205–215.

Beleigoli, A. M., Andrade, A. Q., Cançado, A. G., Paulo, M. N., Diniz, M. F. H., & Ribeiro, A. L. (2019). Web-based digital health interventions for weight loss and lifestyle habit changes in overweight and obese adults: Systematic review and meta-analysis. *Journal of Medical Internet Research*, *21*, e298.

Bendelin, N., Gerdle, B., & Andersson, G. (2024). Hurdles and potentials when implementing internet-delivered acceptance and commitment therapy for chronic pain: A retrospective appraisal using the quality implementation framework. *Scandinavian Journal of Pain*, *24*, 20220139.

Bendelin, N., Hesser, H., Dahl, J., Carlbring, P., Zetterqvist Nelson, K., & Andersson, G. (2011). Experiences of guided Internet-based cognitive-behavioural treatment for depression: A qualitative study. *BMC Psychiatry*, *11*, 107.

Bennett-Levy, J., Thwaites, R., Haarhof, B., & Perry, H. (2015). *Experiencing CBT from the inside out*. Guilford Press.

Bennion, M. R., Hardy, G. E., Moore, R. K., Kellett, S., & Millings, A. (2020). Usability, acceptability, and effectiveness of web-based conversational agents to facilitate problem solving in older adults: Controlled study. *Journal of Medical Internet Research*, *22*, e16794.

Berg, M. (2021). *Just know it: The role of explicit knowledge in internet-based cognitive behaviour therapy for adolescents* (No. 806). Linköping University Electronic Press.

Berg, M., Andersson, G., & Rozental, A. (2020). Knowledge about treatment, anxiety, and depression in association with internet-based cognitive behaviour therapy for adolescents. Development and initial evaluation of a new test. *Sage Open*, *10*.

Berg, M., Klemetz, H., Lindegaard, T., & Andersson, G. (2023). Self-esteem in new light: A qualitative study of experiences of internet-based cognitive behaviour therapy for low self-esteem in adolescents. *BMC Psychiatry*, *23*, 810.

Berg, M., Lindegaard, T., Flygare, A., Sjöbrink, J., Hagvall, L., Palmebäck, S., Klemetz, H., Ludvigsson, M., & Andersson, G. (2022). Internet-based CBT for adolescents with low self-esteem: A pilot randomized controlled trial. *Cognitive Behaviour Therapy*, *51*, 388–407.

Berg, M., Malmqvist, A., Rozental, A., Topooco, N., & Andersson, G. (2020). Knowledge gain and usage of knowledge learned during internet-based CBT treatment for adolescent depression – a qualitative study. *BMC Psychiatry*, *20*, 441.

Berg, M., Rozental, A., de Brun Mangs, J., Näsman, M., Strömberg, K., Viberg, L., Wallner, E., Öhman, H., Silfvernagel, K., Zetterqvist, M.,

Topooco, N., Capusan, A., & Andersson, G. (2020). The role of learning support and chat-sessions in guided internet-based cognitive behavioural therapy for adolescents with anxiety: A factorial design study. *Frontiers in Psychiatry*, *11*, 503.

Berg, M., Rozental, A., Johansson, S., Liljethörn, l., Radvogin, E., Topooco, N., & Andersson, G. (2019). The role of knowledge in Internet-based cognitive behavioural therapy for adolescent depression: Results from a randomised controlled study. *Internet Interventions*, *15*, 10–17.

Berger, T. (2017). The therapeutic alliance in internet interventions: A narrative review and suggestions for future research. *Psychotherapy Research*, *27*, 511–524.

Berger, T., Boettcher, J., & Caspar, F. (2014). Internet-based guided self-help for several anxiety disorders: A randomized controlled trial comparing a tailored with a standardized disorder-specific approach. *Psychotherapy*, *51*, 207–219.

Berger, T., Caspar, F., Richardson, R., Kneubühler, B., Sutter, D., & Andersson, G. (2011). Internet-based treatment of social phobia: A randomized controlled trial comparing unguided with two types of guided self-help. *Behaviour Research and Therapy*, *48*, 158–169.

Bernal, G., Bonilla, J., & Bellido, C. (1995). Ecological validity and cultural sensitivity for outcome research: Issues for the cultural adaptation and development of psychosocial treatments with Hispanics. *Journal of Abnormal Child Psychology*, *23*, 67–82.

Beukes, E. W., Manchaiah, V., Allen, P. M., Baguley, D. M., & Andersson, G. (2019). Internet-based interventions for adults with hearing loss, tinnitus, and vestibular disorders: A systematic review and meta-analysis. *Trends in Hearing*, *23*.

Biliunaite, I., Kazlauskas, E., Sanderman, R., Truskauskaite-Kuneviciene, I., Dumarkaite, A., & Andersson, G. (2021). Internet-based cognitive behavioral therapy for informal caregivers: Randomized controlled pilot trial. *Journal of Medical Internet Research*, *23*, e21466.

Binoy, S., Woody, R., Ivry, R. B., & Saban, W. (2023). Feasibility and efficacy of online neuropsychological assessment. *Sensors*, *23*, 5160.

Bisson, J. I., Ariti, C., Cullen, K., Kitchiner, N., Lewis, C., Roberts, N. P., Simon, N., Smallman, K., Addison, K., Bell, V., Brookes-Howell, L., Cosgrove, S., Ehlers, A., Fitzsimmons, D., Foscarini-Craggs, P., Harris,

S. R. S., Kelson, M., Lovell, K., McKenna, M., . . . Williams-Thomas, R. (2022). Guided, internet based, cognitive behavioural therapy for post-traumatic stress disorder: Pragmatic, multicentre, randomised controlled non-inferiority trial (RAPID). *British Medical Journal, 377*, e069405.

Bjureberg, J., Ojala, O., Berg, A., Edvardsson, E., Kolbeinsson, Ö., Molander, O., Morin, E., Nordgren, L., Palme, K., Särnholm, J., Wedin, L., Rück, C., Gross, J. J., & Hesser, H. (2023). Targeting maladaptive anger with brief therapist-supported internet-delivered emotion regulation treatments: A randomized controlled trial. *Journal of Consulting and Clinical Psychology, 91*, 254–266.

Bjureberg, J., Ojala, O., Hesser, H., Häbel, H., Sahlin, H., Gratz, K. L., Tull, M. T., Claesdotter Knutsson, E., Hedman-Lagerlöf, E., Ljótsson, B., & Hellner, C. (2023). Effect of internet-delivered emotion regulation individual therapy for adolescents with nonsuicidal self-injury disorder: A randomized clinical trial. *JAMA Network Open, 6*, e2322069.

Boberg, J., Kaldo, V., Mataix-Cols, D., Crowley, J. J., Roelstraete, B., Halvorsen, M., Forsell, E., Isacsson, N. H., Sullivan, P. F., Svanborg, C., Andersson, E. H., Lindefors, N., Kravchenko, O., Mattheisen, M., Danielsdottir, H. B., Ivanova, E., Boman, M., Fernández de la Cruz, L., Wallert, J., & Rück, C. (2023). Swedish multimodal cohort of patients with anxiety or depression treated with internet-delivered psychotherapy (MULTI-PSYCH). *BMJ Open, 13*(10), e069427.

Boettcher, J., Leek, L., Matson, L., Holmes, E. A., Browning, M., MacLeod, C., Andersson, G., & Carlbring, P. (2013). Internet-based attention modification for social anxiety: A randomised controlled comparison of training towards negative and training towards positive cues. *PLoS One, 8*, e71760.

Bohman, B., Santi, A., & Andersson, G. (2017). Cognitive-behavioral therapy in practice: Therapist perceptions of techniques, outcome measures, practitioner qualifications, and relation to research. *Cognitive Behaviour Therapy, 46*, 391–403.

Boumparis, N., Loheide-Niesmann, L., Blankers, M., Ebert, D. D., Korf, D., Schaub, M. P., Spijkerman, R., Tait, R. J., & Riper, H. (2019). Short- and long-term effects of digital prevention and treatment interventions for cannabis use reduction: A systematic review and meta-analysis. *Drug and Alcohol Dependence, 200*, 82–94.

Boutron, I., Moher, D., Altman, D. G., Schulz, K. F., & Ravaud, P. (2008). Extending the CONSORT statement to randomized trials of nonpharmacologic treatment: Explanation and elaboration. *Annals of Internal Medicine, 148*, 295–309.

Braun, V., & Clarke, V. (2021). *Thematic analysis: A practical guide*. Sage.

Brewin, C. R. (1996). Theoretical foundations of cognitive-behavior therapy for anxiety and depression. *Annual Review of Psychology, 47*, 33–57.

Buhrman, M., Fältenhag, S., Ström, L., & Andersson, G. (2004). Controlled trial of internet-based treatment with telephone support for chronic back pain. *Pain, 111*, 368–377.

Burns, D. D. (1980). *Feeling good. The new mood therapy*. New American Library.

Carlbring, P., Bohman, S., Brunt, S., Buhrman, M., Westling, B. E., Ekselius, L., & Andersson, G. (2006). Remote treatment of panic disorder: A randomized trial of internet-based cognitive behavioral therapy supplemented with telephone calls. *American Journal of Psychiatry, 163*, 2119–2125.

Carlbring, P., Hadjistavropoulos, H., Kleiboer, A., & Andersson, G. (2023). A new era in Internet interventions: The advent of Chat-GPT and AI-assisted therapist guidance. *Internet Interventions, 32*, 100621.

Carlbring, P., Westling, B. E., Ljungstrand, P., Ekselius, L., & Andersson, G. (2001). Treatment of panic disorder via the internet: A randomized trial of a self-help program. *Behavior Therapy, 32*, 751–764.

Carlson, C. G. (2023). Virtual and augmented simulations in mental health. *Current Psychiatry Reports, 25*, 365–371.

Carnegie, D. (1936). *How to win friends and influence people*. Simon & Schuster.

Cervin, M., & Lundgren, T. (2022). Technology-delivered cognitive-behavioral therapy for pediatric anxiety disorders: A meta-analysis of remission, posttreatment anxiety, and functioning. *Journal of Child Psychology and Psychiatry, 63*, 7–18.

Chen, P. V., Helm, A., Caloudas, S. G., Ecker, A., Day, G., Hogan, J., & Lindsay, J. (2022). Evidence of phone vs video-conferencing for mental health treatments: A review of the literature. *Current Psychiatry Reports*, *24*, 529–539.

Chen, Z., Huang, H., Liu, R., & Tang, Z. (2024). Effects of internet-based exercise intervention on depression and anxiety: A systematic review and meta-analysis. *Medicine*, *103*, e37373.

Choi, I., Zou, J., Titov, N., Dear, B. F., Li, S., Johnston, L., Andrews, G., & Hunt, C. (2012). Culturally attuned internet treatment for depression amongst Chinese Australians: A randomised controlled trial. *Journal of Affective Disorders*, *136*, 459–468.

Clark, D. M. (2004). Developing new treatments: On the interplay between theories, experimental science and clinical innovation. *Behaviour Research and Therapy*, *42*, 1089–1104.

Clark, D. M. (2018). Realizing the mass public benefit of evidence-based psychological therapies: The IAPT program. *Annual Review of Clinical Psychology*, *14*, 159–183.

Clark, D. M., Wild, J., Warnock-Parkes, E., Stott, R., Grey, N., Thew, G., & Ehlers, A. (2023). More than doubling the clinical benefit of each hour of therapist time: A randomised controlled trial of internet cognitive therapy for social anxiety disorder. *Psychological Medicine*, *53*, 5022–5032.

Colombo, D., Fernandez-Alvarez, J., Patane, A., Semonella, M., Kwiatkowska, M., Garcia-Palacios, A., Cipresso, P., Riva, G., & Botella, C. (2019). Current state and future directions of technology-based ecological momentary assessment and intervention for major depressive disorder: A systematic review. *Journal of Clinical Medicine*, *8*, 465.

Cuijpers, P., Noma, H., Karyotaki, E., Vinkers, C. H., Cipriani, A., & Furukawa, T. A. (2020). A network meta-analysis of the effects of psychotherapies, pharmacotherapies and their combination in the treatment of adult depression. *World Psychiatry*, *19*, 92–107.

Dagöö, J., Persson Asplund, R., Andersson Bsenko, H., Hjerling, S., Holmberg, A., Westh, S., Öberg, L., Ljótsson, B., Carlbring, P., Furmark, T., & Andersson, G. (2014). Cognitive behavior therapy versus interpersonal psychotherapy for social anxiety disorder delivered via smartphone and computer: A randomized controlled trial. *Journal of Anxiety Disorders*, *28*, 410–417.

Dahlin, M., Johansson, A., Romare, H., Carlbring, P., & Andersson, G. (2022). Worry-specific versus self-tailored internet-based treatments for generalized anxiety disorder, with scheduled support or support on demand: A pilot factorial design trial. *Internet Interventions, 28*, 100531.

Dear, B. F., Zou, J., Titov, N., Lorian, C., Johnston, L., Spence, J., Anderson, T., Sachdev, P., Brodaty, H., & Knight, R. G. (2013). Internet-delivered cognitive behavioural therapy for depression: A feasibility open trial for older adults. *Australian and New Zealand Journal of Psychiatry, 47*, 169–176.

Demetry, Y., Wasteson, E., Lindegaard, T., Abuleild, A., Geranmaye, A., Andersson, G., & Shahnavaz, S. (2023). Individually tailored and culturally adapted iCBT for Arabic-speaking youth with mental health problems: A mixed methods pilot study in Sweden. *JMIR Formative Research, 7*, e46253.

Dever Fitzgerald, T., Hunter, P. V., Hadjistavropoulos, T., & Koocher, G. P. (2010). Ethical and legal considerations for internet-based psychotherapy. *Cognitive Behaviour Therapy, 39*, 173–187.

Domhardt, M., Letsch, J., Kybelka, J., Koenigbauer, J., Doebler, P., & Baumeister, H. (2020). Are internet- and mobile-based interventions effective in adults with diagnosed panic disorder and/or agoraphobia? A systematic review and meta-analysis. *Journal of Affective Disorders, 276*, 169–182.

Doss, B. D., Knopp, K., Roddy, M. K., Rothman, K., Hatch, S. G., & Rhoades, G. K. (2020). Online programs improve relationship functioning for distressed low-income couples: Results from a nationwide randomized controlled trial. *Journal of Consulting and Clinical Psychology, 88*, 283–294.

Drummond, M. F., Sculpher, M. J., Torrance, G. W., O'Brien, B. J., & Stoddart, G. L. (2005). *Methods for the economic evaluation of health care programmes* (3rd ed.). Oxford University Press.

Dworschak, C., Heim, E., & Maercker, A. (2022). Efficacy of internet-based interventions for common mental disorder symptoms and psychosocial problems in older adults: A systematic review and meta-analysis. *Internet Interventions, 27*, 100498.

Ebert, D. D., Lehr, F., Boß, L., Riper, H., Cuijpers, P., Andersson, G., Thiart, H., Heber, E., & Berking, M. (2014). Efficacy of an internet-based problem-solving training for teachers: Results of a randomized controlled trial. *Scandinavian Journal of Work, Environment & Health*, *40*, 582–596.

Ebert, D. D., Zarski, A. C., Christensen, H., Stikkelbroek, Y., Cuijpers, P., Berking, M., & Riper, H. (2015). Internet and computer-based cognitive behavioral therapy for anxiety and depression in youth: A meta-analysis of randomized controlled outcome trials. *PLoS One, 10*, e0119895.

Edmonds, M., McCall, H., Dear, B. F., Titov, N., & Hadjistavropoulos, H. D. (2020). Does concurrent medication usage affect patient response to internet-delivered cognitive behaviour therapy for depression and anxiety? *Internet Interventions, 19*, 100302.

Ehlers, A., Wild, J., Warnock-Parkes, E., Grey, N., Murray, H., Kerr, A., Rozental, A., Thew, G., Janecka, M., Beierl, E. T., Tsiachristas, A., Perera-Salazar, R., Andersson, G., & Clark, D. M. (2023). Therapist-assisted online psychological therapies differing in trauma focus for post-traumatic stress disorder (STOP-PTSD): A UK-based, single-blind, randomised controlled trial. *Lancet Psychiatry, 10*, 608–622.

Eilert, N., Enrique, A., Wogan, R., Mooney, O., Timulak, L., & Richards, D. (2021). The effectiveness of internet-delivered treatment for generalized anxiety disorder: An updated systematic review and meta-analysis. *Depression and Anxiety, 38*, 196–219.

Enander, J., Andersson, E., Mataix-Cols, D., Lichtenstein, L., Alström, K., Andersson, G., Ljótsson, B., & Rück, C. (2016). Therapist guided internet based cognitive behavioural therapy for body dysmorphic disorder: Single blind randomised controlled trial. *British Medical Journal, 352*, i241.

Epstein, J., & Klinkenberg, W. D. (2001). From Eliza to internet: A brief history of computerized assessment. *Computers in Human Behavior, 17*, 295–314.

Erbe, D., Eichert, H. C., Riper, H., & Ebert, D. D. (2017). Blending face-to-face and internet-based interventions for the treatment of mental disorders in adults: Systematic review. *Journal of Medical Internet Research, 19*, e306.

Etzelmueller, A., Vis, C., Karyotaki, E., Baumeister, H., Titov, N., Berking, M., Cuijpers, P., Riper, H., & Ebert, D. D. (2020). Effects of Internet-based cognitive behavioral therapy in routine care for adults in treatment for depression and anxiety: Systematic review and meta-analysis. *Journal of Medical Internet Research, 22*, e18100.

Eysenbach, G. (2005). The law of attrition. *Journal of Medical Internet Research, 7*(1), e11.

Farvolden, P., Denisoff, E., Selby, P., Bagby, R. M., & Rudy, L. (2005). Usage and longitudinal effectiveness of a web-based self-help cognitive behavioral therapy program for panic disorder. *Journal of Medical Internet Research, 7*(1), e7.

Fleming, T. M., Bavin, L., Stasiak, K., Hermansson-Webb, E., Merry, S. N., Cheek, C., Lucassen, M., Lau, H. M., Pollmuller, B., & Hetrick, S. (2016). Serious games and gamification for mental health: Current status and promising directions. *Frontiers in Psychiatry, 7*, 215.

Furmark, T., Carlbring, P., Hedman, E., Sonnenstein, A., Clevberger, P., Bohman, B., Eriksson, A., Hållén, A., Frykman, M., Holmström, A., Sparthan, E., Tillfors, M., Nilsson Ihrfelt, E., Spak, M., Eriksson, A., Ekselius, L., & Andersson, G. (2009). Guided and unguided self-help for social anxiety disorder: Randomised controlled trial. *British Journal of Psychiatry, 195*, 440–447.

Gandy, M., Karin, E., McDonald, S., Meares, S., Scott, A. J., Titov, N., & Dear, B. F. (2020). A feasibility trial of an internet-delivered psychological intervention to manage mental health and functional outcomes in neurological disorders. *Journal of Psychosomatic Research, 136*, 110173.

Gandy, M., Pang, S. T. Y., Scott, A. J., Heriseanu, A. I., Bisby, M. A., Dudeney, J., Karin, E., Titov, N., & Dear, B. F. (2022). Internet-delivered cognitive and behavioural based interventions for adults with chronic pain: A systematic review and meta-analysis of randomized controlled trials. *Pain, 163*, e1041–e1053.

Gold, S. M., Friede, T., Meyer, B., Moss-Morris, R., Hudson, J., Asseyer, S., Bellmann-Strobl, J., Leisdon, A., Ißels, L., Ritter, K., Schymainski, D., Pomeroy, H., Lynch, S. G., Cozart, J. S., Thelen, J., Román, C. A. F., Cadden, M., Guty, E., Lau, S., . . . Heesen, C. (2023). Internet-delivered cognitive behavioural therapy programme to reduce depressive symptoms in patients with multiple sclerosis: A multicentre, randomised, controlled, phase 3 trial. *Lancet Digit Health*, *5*, e668–e678.

Greist, J. H., Gustafson, D. H., Stauss, F. F., Rowse, G. L., Laughren, T. P., & Chiles, J. A. (1973). A computer interview for suicide-risk prediction. *American Journal of Psychiatry*, *130*, 1327–1332.

Greist, J. H., Marks, I. M., Baer, L., Kobak, K. A., Wenzel, K. W., Hirsch, J., Mantle, J. M., & Clary, C. M. (2002). Behavior therapy for obsessive-compulsive disorder guided by a computer or by a clinician compared with relaxation as a control. *Journal of Clinical Psychiatry*, *62*, 138–145.

Guo, S., Deng, W., Wang, H., Liu, J., Liu, X., Yang, X., He, C., Zhang, Q., Liu, B., Dong, X., Yang, Z., Li, Z., & Li, X. (2021). The efficacy of internet-based cognitive behavioural therapy for social anxiety disorder: A systematic review and meta-analysis. *Clinical Psychology & Psychotherapy*, *28*, 656–668.

Gürses, E., Beukes, E., Cesur, S., Andersson, G., & Manchaiah, V. (2023). A comparative study of readability, acceptability, and the adaptation of an internet-based cognitive behavioral therapy for tinnitus. *Journal of International Advanced Otology*, *19*, 182–190.

Hadjistavropoulos, H. D., Gullickson, K. M., Schneider, L. H., Dear, B. F., & Titov, N. (2019). Development of the internet-delivered cognitive behaviour therapy undesirable therapist behaviours scale (ICBT-UTBS). *Internet Interventions*, *18*, 100255.

Halaj, A., Strauss, A. Y., Zalaznik, D., Fradkin, I., Zlotnick, E., Andersson, G., Ebert, D. D., & Huppert, J. D. (2023). Examining the relationship between cognitive factors and insight in panic disorder before and during treatment. *Cognitive Behaviour Therapy*, *52*, 331–346.

Haller, K., Becker, P., Niemeyer, H., & Boettcher, J. (2023). Who benefits from guided internet-based interventions? A systematic review of predictors and moderators of treatment outcome. *Internet Interventions*, *33*, 100635.

Hamid, N. (2024). Internet-based cognitive behaviour therapy for the prevention, treatment and relapse prevention of eating disorders: A systematic review and meta-analysis. *PsyCh Journal*, *13*, 5–18.

Han, A., & Kim, T. H. (2022). Efficacy of internet-based acceptance and commitment therapy for depressive symptoms, anxiety, stress, psychological distress, and quality of life: Systematic review and meta-analysis. *Journal of Medical Internet Research*, *24*, e39727.

Harvey, A. G., Lee, J., Williams, J., Hollon, S. D., Walker, M. P., Thompson, M. A., & Smith, R. (2014). Improving outcome of psychosocial treatments by enhancing memory and learning. *Perspectives on Psychological Science*, *9*, 161–179.

Hattie, J. (2009). *Visible learning. A synthesis of over 800 meta-analyses relating to achievement*. Routledge.

Hedman-Lagerlöf, E., Carlbring, P., Svärdman, F., Riper, H., Cuijpers, P., & Andersson, G. (2023). Therapist-supported Internet-based cognitive behaviour therapy yields similar effects as face-to-face therapy for psychiatric and somatic disorders: An updated systematic review and meta-analysis. *World Psychiatry*, *25*, 305–314.

Heim, E., Rötger, A., Lorenz, N., & Maercker, A. (2018). Working alliance with an avatar: How far can we go with internet interventions? *Internet Interventions*, *11*, 41–46.

Hertel, P. T., & Mathews, A. (2011). Cognitive bias modification: Past perspectives, current findings, and future applications. *Perspectives on Psychological Science*, *6*, 521–536.

Hesser, H., Axelsson, S., Bäcke, V., Engstrand, J., Gustafsson, T., Holmgren, E., Jeppsson, U., Pollack, M., Norden, K., Rosenqvist, D., & Andersson, G. (2017). Preventing intimate partner violence via the internet: A randomized controlled trial of emotion-regulation and conflict-management training for individuals with aggression problems. *Clinical Psychology & Psychotherapy*, *24*, 1163–1177.

Hill, C., Creswell, C., Vigerland, S., Nauta, M. H., March, S., Donovan, C., Wolters, L., Spence, S. H., Martin, J. L., Wozney, L., McLellan, L., Kreuze, L., Gould, K., Jolstedt, M., Nord, M., Hudson, J. L., Utens, E., Ruwaard, J., Albers, C., . . . Kendall, P. C. (2018). Navigating the development and dissemination of internet cognitive behavioral therapy (iCBT) for anxiety disorders in children and young people: A consensus statement with recommendations from the #iCBTLorentz Workshop Group. *Internet Interventions*, *12*, 1–10.

Holländare, F., Johnsson, S., Randestad, M., Tillfors, M., Carlbring, P., Andersson, G., & Engström, I. (2011). Randomized trial of internet-based relapse prevention for partially remitted depression. *Acta Psychiatrica Scandinavica, 124*, 285–294.

Iliakis, E. A., & Masland, S. R. (2023). Internet interventions for perfectionism: A meta-analysis and proposals for the college setting. *Journal of American College Health, 71*, 2299–2304.

International Test Commission and Association of Test Publishers. (2022). *Guidelines for technology-based assessment.* www.intestcom.org/page/28

Jackson, H. M., Calear, A. L., Batterham, P. J., Ohan, J. L., Farmer, G. M., & Farrer, L. M. (2023). Skill enactment and knowledge acquisition in digital cognitive behavioral therapy for depression and anxiety: Systematic review of randomized controlled trials. *Journal of Medical Internet Research, 25*, e44673.

Jacobi, C., Vollert, B., Kristian, H., von Bloh, P., Eiterich, N., Gorlich, D., & Taylor, C. B. (2023). Indicated, internet-based prevention for women with anorexia nervosa symptoms: A randomised controlled efficacy trial. *Journal of Medical Internet Research, 24*, e35947.

Janse, A., Worm-Smeitink, M., Bleijenberg, G., Donders, R., & Knoop, H. (2018). Efficacy of web-based cognitive-behavioural therapy for chronic fatigue syndrome: Randomised controlled trial. *British Journal of Psychiatry, 212*, 112–118.

Johansson, M., Romero, D., Jakobson, M., Heinemans, N., & Lindner, P. (2024). Digital interventions targeting excessive substance use and substance use disorders: A comprehensive and systematic scoping review and bibliometric analysis. *Frontiers in Psychiatry, 15*, 1233888.

Johansson, O., Michel, T., Andersson, G., & Paxling, B. (2015). Experiences of non-adherence to internet-delivered cognitive behaviour therapy: A qualitative study. *Internet Interventions, 2*, 137–142.

Johansson, P., Lundgren, J., Andersson, G., Svensson, E., & Mourad, G. (2022). Internet-based cognitive behavioral therapy and its association with self-efficacy, depressive symptoms, and physical activity: Secondary analysis of a randomized controlled trial in patients with cardiovascular disease. *JMIR Cardio, 6*, e29926.

Johansson, P., Westas, M., Andersson, G., Alehagen, U., Broström, A., Jaarsma, T., Mourad, G., & Lundgren, J. (2019). An internet-based cognitive behavioral therapy program adapted to patients with cardio-vascular disease and depression: Randomized controlled trial. *JMIR Mental Health*, *6*, e14648.

Johansson, R., & Andersson, G. (2012). Internet-based psychological treatments for depression. *Expert Review of Neurotherapeutics*, *12*, 861–870.

Johansson, R., Nyblom, A., Carlbring, P., Cuijpers, P., & Andersson, G. (2013). Choosing between internet-based psychodynamic versus cognitive behavioral therapy for depression: A pilot preference study. *BMC Psychiatry*, *13*, 268.

Jolstedt, M., Ljótsson, B., Fredlander, S., Tedgård, T., Hallberg, A., Ekeljung, A., Högström, J., Mataix-Cols, D., Serlachius, E., & Vigerland, S. (2018). Implementation of internet-delivered CBT for children with anxiety disorders in a rural area: A feasibility trial. *Internet Interventions*, *12*, 121–129.

Jones, E. B., & Sharpe, L. (2017). Cognitive bias modification: A review of meta-analyses. *Journal of Affective Disorders*, *223*, 175–183.

Jones, S. L., Hadjistavropoulos, H. D., & Soucy, J. N. (2016). A randomized controlled trial of guided internet-delivered cognitive behaviour therapy for older adults with generalized anxiety. *Journal of Anxiety Disorders*, *37*, 1–9.

Kählke, F., Buntrock, C., Smit, F., & Ebert, D. D. (2022). Systematic review of economic evaluations for internet- and mobile-based interventions for mental health problems. *npj Digital Medicine*, *5*, 175.

Kaiser, J., Hanschmidt, F., & Kersting, A. (2021). The association between therapeutic alliance and outcome in internet-based psychological interventions: A meta-analysis. *Computers in Human Behavior*, *114*, 106512.

Käll, A., & Andersson, G. (2023). Knowledge acquisition following internet-based cognitive behavioural therapy for loneliness – A secondary analysis of a randomised controlled trial. *Journal of Behavior Therapy and Experimental Psychiatry*, *81*, 101872.

Käll, A., Bäck, M., Welin, C., Åman, H., Bjerkander, R., Wänman, M., Lindegaard, T., Berg, M., Moche, H., Shafran, R., & Andersson, G. (2021). Therapist guided internet-based treatments for loneliness:

A randomised controlled three-arm trial comparing cognitive behavioural therapy and interpersonal psychotherapy. *Psychotherapy and Psychosomatics, 90*, 351–358.

Käll, A., Olsson Lynch, C., Sundling, K., Furmark, T., Carlbring, P., & Andersson, G. (2023). Scheduled support versus support on demand in internet-delivered cognitive behavioral therapy for social anxiety disorder: Randomized controlled trial. *Clinical Psychology in Europe, 5*, e11379.

Kambeitz-Ilankovic, L., Rzayeva, U., Völkel, L., Wenzel, J., Weiske, J., Jessen, F., Reininghaus, U., Uhlhaas, P. J., Alvarez-Jimenez, M., & Kambeitz, J. (2022). A systematic review of digital and face-to-face cognitive behavioral therapy for depression. *npj Digital Medicine, 5*, 144.

Karyotaki, E., Ebert, D. D., Donkin, L., Riper, H., Twisk, J., Burger, S., Rozental, A., Lange, A., Williams, A. D., Zarski, A. C., Geraedts, A., van Straten, A., Kleiboer, A., Meyer, B., Ince, B. Ü., Buntrock, C., Lehr, D., Snoek, F. J., Andrews, G., . . . Cuijpers, P. (2018). Do guided internet-based interventions result in clinically relevant changes for patients with depression? An individual participant data meta-analysis. *Clinical Psychology Review, 63*, 80–92.

Kazdin, A. E. (2007). Mediators and mechanisms of change in psychotherapy research. *Annual Review of Clinical Psychology, 3*, 1–27.

Keeley, H., Williams, C., & Shapiro, D. A. (2002). A United Kingdom survey of accredited cognitive behaviour therapists' attitudes towards and use of structured self-help materials. *Behavioural and Cognitive Psychotherapy, 30*, 193–203.

Kenwright, M., Marks, I., Graham, C., Franses, A., & Mataix-Cols, D. (2005). Brief scheduled phone support from a clinician to enhance computer-aided self-help for obsessive-compulsive disorder: Randomized controlled trial. *Journal of Clinical Psychology, 61*, 1499–1508.

Kim, H., Oh, Y., & Chang, S. J. (2022). Internet-delivered cognitive behavioral therapy in patients with irritable bowel syndrome: Systematic review and meta-analysis. *Journal of Medical Internet Research, 24*, e35260.

Kjell, O. N. E., Kjell, K., Garcia, D., & Sikström, S. (2019). Semantic measures: Using natural language processing to measure, differentiate, and describe psychological constructs. *Psychological Methods*, *24*, 92–115.

Knaevelsrud, C., Böttche, M., Pietrzak, R. H., Freyberger, H. J., & Kuwert, P. (2017). Efficacy and feasibility of a therapist-guided internet-based Intervention for older persons with childhood traumatization: A randomized controlled trial. *American Journal of Geriatric Psychiatry*, *25*, 878–888.

Koelen, J. A., Vonk, A., Klein, A., de Koning, L., Vonk, P., de Vet, S., & Wiers, R. (2022). Man vs. machine: A meta-analysis on the added value of human support in text-based internet treatments ("e-therapy") for mental disorders. *Clinical Psychology Review*, *96*, 102179.

Komariah, M., Amirah, S., Faisal, E. G., Prayogo, S. A., Maulana, S., Platini, H., Suryani, S., Yosep, I., & Arifin, H. (2022). Efficacy of internet-based cognitive behavioral therapy for depression and anxiety among global population during the COVID-19 pandemic: A systematic review and meta-analysis of a randomized controlled trial study. *Healthcare*, *10*, 1224.

Königbauer, J., Letsch, J., Doebler, P., Ebert, D., & Baumeister, H. (2017). Internet- and mobile-based depression interventions for people with diagnosed depression: A systematic review and meta-analysis. *Journal of Affective Disorders*, *223*, 28–40.

Krieger, T., Reber, F., von Glutz, B., Urech, A., Moser, C. T., Schulz, A., & Berger, T. (2019). An internet-based compassion-focused intervention for increased self-criticism: A randomized controlled trial. *Behavior Therapy*, *50*, 430–445.

Lange, A., van den Ven, J.-P., Schrieken, B., & Emmelkamp, P. M. G. (2001). Interapy, treatment of posttraumatic stress through the internet: A controlled trial. *Journal of Behavior Therapy and Experimental Psychiatry*, *32*, 73–90.

Lätth, J., Landgren, V., McMahan, A., Sparre, C., Eriksson, J., Malki, K., Söderquist, E., Görts Öberg, K., Rozental, A., Andersson, G., Kaldo, V., Långström, N., & Rahm, C. (2022). Effects of internet-delivered cognitive behavioral therapy on use of child sexual abuse material:

A randomized placebo-controlled trial on the Darknet. *Internet Interventions*, *30*, 100590.

Lenhard, F., Andersson, E., Mataix-Cols, D., Ruck, C., Vigerland, S., Hogstrom, J., Hillborg, M., Brander, G., Ljungstrom, M., Ljotsson, B., & Serlachius, E. (2017). Therapist-guided, internet-delivered cognitive-behavioral therapy for adolescents with obsessive-compulsive disorder: A randomized controlled trial. *Journal of the American Academy of Child and Adolescent Psychiatry*, *56*, 10–19.e12.

Lewinsohn, P. M., Munoz, R. F., Youngren, M. A., & Zeiss, M. A. (1986). *Control your depression*. Prentice Hall.

Lewis, C., Roberts, N. P., Simon, N., Bethell, A., & Bisson, J. I. (2019). Internet-delivered cognitive behavioural therapy for post-traumatic stress disorder: Systematic review and meta-analysis. *Acta Psychiatrica Scandinavica*, *140*, 508–521.

Linardon, J., Broadbent, J., Shatte, A., & Fuller-Tyszkiewicz, M. (2022). The role of pre-existing knowledge and knowledge acquisition in internet-based cognitive-behavioural therapy for eating disorders. *Computers in Human Behavior*, *134*, 107332.

Lindegaard, T., Berg, M., & Andersson, G. (2020). Efficacy of internet-delivered psychodynamic therapy: Systematic review and meta-analysis. *Psychodynamic Psychiatry*, *48*, 437–454.

Lindegaard, T., Brohede, D., Koshnawa, K., Osmana, S. S., Johansson, R., & Andersson, G. (2019). Internet-based treatment of depressive symptoms in a Kurdish population: A randomized controlled trial. *Journal of Clinical Psychology*, *75*, 985–998.

Lindh-Åstrand, L., Spetz Holm, A.-C., Sydsjö, G., Andersson, G., Carlbring, P., & Nedstrand, E. (2015). Internet-delivered applied relaxation for vasomotor symptoms in postmenopausal women: Lessons from a failed trial. *Maturitas*, *80*, 432–434.

Lindhe, N., Bengtsson, A., Byggeth, E., Engström, J., Lundin, M., Ludvigsson, M., Aminoff, V., Berg, M., & Andersson, G. (2023). Tailored internet-delivered cognitive behavioral therapy for individuals experiencing psychological distress associated with climate change: A pilot randomized controlled trial. *Behaviour Research and Therapy*, *171*, 104438.

Lindner, P., Miloff, A., Hamilton, W., Reuterskiöld, L., Andersson, G., Powers, M., & Carlbring, P. (2017). Creating state of the art, next-generation Virtual Reality exposure therapies for anxiety disorders using consumer hardware platforms: Design considerations and future direction. *Cognitive Behaviour Therapy, 46*, 404–420.

Ljótsson, B., Hesser, H., Andersson, E., Lindfors, P.-J., Hursti, T., Rück, C., Lindefors, N., Andersson, G., & Hedman, E. (2013). Mechanisms of change in exposure-based internet-treatment for irritable bowel syndrome. *Journal of Consulting and Clinical Psychology, 81*, 1113–1126.

Ludden, G. D., van Rompay, T. J., Kelders, S. M., & van Gemert-Pijnen, J. E. (2015). How to increase reach and adherence of web-based interventions: A design research viewpoint. *Journal of Medical Internet Research, 17*, e172.

Lundgren, J., Johansson, P., Jaarsma, T., Andersson, G., & Kärner Köhler, A. (2018). Patients' experiences of web-based cognitive behavioral therapy for heart failure and depression: Qualitative study. *Journal of Medical Internet Research, 20*, e10302.

Ly, K. H., Trüschel, A., Jarl, L., Magnusson, S., Windahl, T., Johansson, R., Carlbring, P., & Andersson, G. (2014). Behavioral activation vs. Mindfulness-based guided self-help treatment administered through a smartphone application: A randomized controlled trial. *BMJ Open, 4*, e003440.

Ma, L., Mor, S., Anderson, P. L., Baños, R. M., Botella, C., Bouchard, S., Cárdenas-López, G., Donker, T., Fernández-Álvarez, J., Lindner, P., Mühlberger, A., Powers, M. B., Quero, S., Rothbaum, B., Wiederhold, B. K., & Carlbring, P. (2021). Integrating virtual realities and psychotherapy: SWOT analysis on VR and MR based treatments of anxiety and stress-related disorders. *Cognitive Behaviour Therapy, 50*, 509–526.

Machado-Sousa, M., Moreira, P. S., Costa, A. D., Soriano-Mas, C., & Morgado, P. (2023). Efficacy of internet-based cognitive-behavioral therapy for obsessive-compulsive disorder: A systematic review and meta-analysis. *Clinical Psychology: Science and Practice, 30*, 150–162.

Maj, A., Matyni, M., Michalak, N., Bis, A., & Andersson, G. (2024). New in Town – An internet-based self-efficacy intervention for internal migrants: A randomized controlled trial. *PLoS One, 19*, e0299638.

Månsson, K. N. T., Carlbring, P., Frick, A., Engman, A., Olsson, C. J., Bodlund, O., Furmark, T., & Andersson, G. (2013). Altered neural correlates of affective processing after internet-delivered cognitive behavior therapy for social anxiety disorder. *Psychiatry Research: Neuroimaging, 214*, 229–237.

Månsson, K. N. T., Lindqvist, D., Yang, L., Svanborg, C., Isung, J., Nilsonne, G., Bergman Nordgren, L., El Alaoui, S., Hedman-Lagerlöf, E., Kraepelien, M., Högström, J., Andersson, G., Boraxbekk, C.-J., Fischer, H., Lavebratt, C., Wolkowitz, O., & Furmark, T. (2019). Improvement in indices of cellular protection after psychological treatment for social anxiety disorder. *Translational Psychiatry, 9*, 340.

Månsson, K. N. T., Ruiz, E., Gervind, E., Dahlin, M., & Andersson, G. (2013). Development and initial evaluation of an Internet-based support system for face to face cognitive behavior therapy: A proof of concept study. *Journal of Medical Internet Research, 15*, e280.

Månsson, K. N. T., Salami, A., Carlbring, P., Boraxbekk, C.-J., Andersson, G., & Furmark, T. (2017). Structural but not functional neuroplasticity one year after effective cognitive behaviour therapy for social anxiety disorders. *Behavioural Brain Research, 318*, 45–51.

March, S., Donovan, C. L., Baldwin, S., Ford, M., & Spence, S. H. (2019). Using stepped-care approaches within internet-based interventions for youth anxiety: Three case studies. *Internet Interventions, 18*, 100281.

Marks, I. M., Cavanagh, K., & Gega, L. (2007). *Hands-on help. Computer-aided psychotherapy.* Psychology Press.

Marks, I. M., Kenwright, M., McDonough, M., Whittaker, M., & Mataix-Cols, D. (2004). Saving clinicians' time by delegating routine aspects of therapy to a computer: A randomized controlled trial in phobia/panic disorder. *Psychological Medicine, 34*, 9–18.

Marrs, R. W. (1995). A meta-analysis of bibliotherapy studies. *American Journal of Community Psychology, 23*, 843–870.

Martin-Key, N. A., Spadaro, B., Funnell, E., Barker, E. J., Schei, T. S., Tomasik, J., & Bahn, S. (2022). The current state and validity of digital assessment tools for psychiatry: Systematic review. *JMIR Mental Health, 9*, e32824.

McAloon, J., & de la Poer Beresford, K. (2023). Online behavioral parenting interventions for disruptive behavioral disorders: A PRISMA based systematic review of clinical trials. *Child Psychiatry and Human Development, 54*, 379–396.

McLellan, L. F., Woon, S., Hudson, J. L., Lyneham, H. J., Karin, E., & Rapee, R. M. (2024). Treating child anxiety using family-based internet delivered cognitive behavior therapy with brief therapist guidance: A randomized controlled trial. *Journal of Anxiety Disorders, 101*, 102802.

Mechler, J., Lindqvist, K., Carlbring, P., Topooco, N., Falkenström, F., Lilliengren, P., Andersson, G., Johansson, R., Midgley, N., Edbrooke-Childs, J. J., Dahl, H.-S., Sandell, R., Thorén, A., Ulberg, R., Lindert Bergsten, K., & Philips, B. (2022). Therapist-guided internet-based psychodynamic therapy versus cognitive behavioural therapy for adolescent depression in Sweden: A randomised, clinical, non-inferiority trial. *Lancet Digital Health, 4*, e594–e603.

Mehrotra, S., Sudhir, P., Rao, G., Thirthalli, J., & Srikanth, T. K. (2018). Development and pilot testing of an internet-based self-help intervention for depression for Indian users. *Behavioral Sciences, 8*, 36.

Mehta, S., Peynenburg, V. A., & Hadjistavropoulos, H. D. (2019). Internet-delivered cognitive behaviour therapy for chronic health conditions: A systematic review and meta-analysis. *Journal of Behavioral Medicine, 42*, 169–187.

Mehta, S. H., Nugent, M., Peynenburg, V., Thiessen, D., La Posta, G., Titov, N., Dear, B. F., & Hadjistavropoulos, H. D. (2022). Internet-delivered cognitive behaviour therapy for chronic health conditions: Self-guided versus team-guided. *Journal of Behavioral Medicine, 45*, 674–689.

Merry, S. N., Stasiak, K., Shepherd, M., Frampton, C., Fleming, T., & Lucassen, M. F. (2012). The effectiveness of SPARX, a computerised self help intervention for adolescents seeking help for depression: Randomised controlled non-inferiority trial. *British Medical Journal, 344*, e2598.

Mewton, L., Sachdev, P. S., & Andrews, G. (2013). A naturalistic study of the acceptability and effectiveness of internet-delivered cognitive behavioural therapy for psychiatric disorders in older Australians. *PLoS One, 8*, e71825.

Miloff, A., Lindner, P., Dafgård, P., Deak, S., Garke, M., Hamilton, W., Heinsoo, J., Kristoffersson, G., Rafi, J., Sindermark, K., Sjölund, J., Zenger, M., Reuterskiöld, L., Andersson, G., & Carlbring, P. (2019). Automated virtual reality exposure therapy for spider phobia vs. in-vivo one-session treatment: A randomized non-inferiority trial. *Behaviour Research and Therapy*, *118*, 130–140.

Mohr, D. C., Cuijpers, P., & Lehman, K. (2011). Supportive accountability: A model for providing human support to enhance adherence to eHealth interventions. *Journal of Medical Internet Research*, *13*(1), e30.

Mohr, D. C., Zhang, M., & Schueller, S. M. (2017). Personal sensing: Understanding mental health using ubiquitous sensors and machine learning. *Annual Review of Clinical Psychology*, *13*, 23–47.

Mor, S., Grimaldos, J., Tur, C., Miguel, C., Cuijpers, P., Botella, C., & Quero, S. (2021). Internet- and mobile-based interventions for the treatment of specific phobia: A systematic review and preliminary meta-analysis. *Internet Interventions*, *26*, 100462.

Morgan, P. J., Lubans, D. R., Collins, C. E., Warren, J. M., & Callister, R. (2009). The SHED-IT randomized controlled trial: Evaluation of an Internet-based weight-loss program for men. *Obesity*, *17*, 2025–2032.

Moshe, I., Terhorst, Y., Philippi, P., Domhardt, M., Cuijpers, P., Cristea, I., Pulkki-Råback, L., Baumeister, H., & Sander, L. B. (2021). Digital interventions for the treatment of depression: A meta-analytic review. *Psychological Bulletin*, *147*, 749–786.

Mourad, G., Lundgren, J., Andersson, G., Husberg, M., & Johansson, P. (2022). Cost-effectiveness of internet-delivered cognitive behavioural therapy in patients with cardiovascular disease and depressive symptoms. Secondary analysis of a RCT. *BMJ Open*, *12*, e059939.

Munoz, R. F. (2010). Using evidence-based internet interventions to reduce health disparities worldwide. *Journal of Medical Internet Research*, 12, e60.

Newman, M. G., Kenardy, J., Herman, S., & Taylor, C. B. (1997). Comparison of palmtop-computer-assisted brief cognitive-behavioral treatment to cognitive-behavioral treatment for panic disorder. *Journal of Consulting and Clinical Psychology*, *65*, 178–183.

Nielssen, O., Staples, L., Karin, E., Kayrouz, R., Dear, B., & Titov, N. (2023). Effectiveness of internet delivered cognitive behaviour therapy provided as routine care for people in the depressed phase of bipolar disorder treated with Lithium. *PLoS Digital Health*, *2*, e0000194.

Nilsen, P. (2015). Making sense of implementation theories, models and frameworks. *Implementation Science*, *10*, 53.

Nomeikaite, A., Gelezelyte, O., Berger, T., Andersson, G., & Kazlauskas, E. (2023). Exploring reasons for usage discontinuation in an internet-delivered stress recovery intervention: A qualitative study. *Internet Interventions*, *34*, 100686.

Nordh, M., Wahlund, T., Jolstedt, M., Sahlin, H., Bjureberg, J., Ahlen, J., Lalouni, M., Salomonsson, S., Vigerland, S., Lavner, M., Öst, L. G., Lenhard, F., Hesser, H., Mataix-Cols, D., Högström, J., & Serlachius, E. (2021). Therapist-guided internet-delivered cognitive behavioral therapy vs internet-delivered supportive therapy for children and adolescents with social anxiety disorder: A randomized clinical trial. *JAMA Psychiatry*, *78*, 705–713.

Nordin, S., Carlbring, P., Cuijpers, P., & Andersson, G. (2010). Expanding the limits of bibliotherapy for panic disorder. Randomized trial of self-help without support but with a clear deadline. *Behavior Therapy*, *41*, 267–276.

Nyström, M. B. T., Stenling, A., Sjöström, E., Neely, G., Lindner, P., Hassmén, P., Andersson, G., Martell, C., & Carlbring, P. (2017). Behavioral activation versus physical activity via the internet: A randomized controlled trial. *Journal of Affective Disorders*, *215*, 85–93.

Oinas-Kukkonen, H., & Harjumaa, M. (2009). Persuasive systems design: Key issues, process model, and system features. *Communications of the Association for Information Systems*, *24*, 28.

Păsărelu, C., Andersson, G., Bergman Nordgren, L., & Dobrean, A. (2017). Internet-delivered transdiagnostic and tailored cognitive behavioral therapy for anxiety and depression: A systematic review and meta-analysis. *Cognitive Behaviour Therapy*, *46*, 1–28.

Patel, S., Akhtar, A., Malins, S., Wright, N., Rowley, E., Young, E., Sampson, S., & Morriss, R. (2020). The acceptability and usability of digital health interventions for adults with depression, anxiety, and somatoform disorders: Qualitative systematic review and meta-synthesis. *Journal of Medical Internet Research*, *22*, e16228.

Paxling, B., Lundgren, S., Norman, A., Almlöv, J., Carlbring, P., Cuijpers, P., & Andersson, G. (2013). Therapist behaviours in Internet-delivered cognitive behaviour therapy: Analyses of e-mail correspondence in the treatment of generalized anxiety disorder. *Behavioural and Cognitive Psychotherapy*, *41*, 280–289.

Proudfoot, J., Swain, S., Widmer, S., Watkins, E., Goldberg, D., Marks, I., Mann, A., & Gray, J. A. (2003). The development and beta-test of a computer-therapy program for anxiety and depression: Hurdles and lessons. *Computers in Human Behavior*, *19*, 277–289.

Richardson, T., Enrique, A., Earley, C., Adegoke, A., Hiscock, D., & Richards, D. (2022). The acceptability and initial effectiveness of "Space from Money Worries": An online cognitive behavioral therapy intervention to tackle the link between financial difficulties and poor mental health. *Frontiers in Public Health*, *10*, 739381.

Ritterband, L. M., Gonder-Frederick, L. A., Cox, D. J., Clifton, A. D., West, R. W., & Borowitz, S. M. (2003). Internet interventions: In review, in use, and into the future. *Professional Psychology: Research and Practice*, *34*, 527–534.

Ritterband, L. M., Thorndike, F. P., Cox, D. J., Kovatchev, B. P., & Gonder-Frederick, L. A. (2009). A behavior change model for internet interventions. *Annals of Behavioral Medicine*, *38*, 18–27.

Rosen, G. M. (1987). Self-help treatment books and the commercialization of psychotherapy. *American Psychologist*, *42*, 46–51.

Rozental, A., Andersson, G., Boettcher, J., Ebert, D., Cuijpers, P., Knaevelsrud, C., Ljótsson, B., Kaldo, V., Titov, N., & Carlbring, P. (2014). Consensus statement on defining and measuring negative effects of Internet interventions. *Internet Interventions*, *1*, 12–19.

Rozental, A., Andersson, G., & Carlbring, P. (2019). In the absence of effects: An individual patient data meta-analysis of non-response and its predictors in internet-based cognitive behavior therapy. *Frontiers in Psychology*, *10*, 589.

Rozental, A., Forsell, E., Svensson, A., Andersson, G., & Carlbring, P. (2015). Internet-based cognitive behavior therapy for procrastination: A randomized controlled trial. *Journal of Consulting and Clinical Psychology*, *83*, 808–824.

Rozental, A., Forsström, D., Lindner, P., Nilsson, S., Mårtensson, L., Rizzo, A., Andersson, G., & Carlbring, P. (2018). Treating procrastination using cognitive behavior therapy: A pragmatic randomized controlled trial comparing treatment delivered via the internet or in groups. *Behavior Therapy*, *49*, 180–197.

Rozental, A., Magnusson, K., Boettcher, J., Andersson, G., & Carlbring, P. (2017). For better or worse: An individual patient data meta-analysis of deterioration among participants receiving internet-based cognitive behavior therapy. *Journal of Consulting and Clinical Psychology, 85,* 160–177.

Ryan, C., Bergin, M., & Wells, J. S. (2018). Theoretical perspectives of adherence to web-based interventions: A scoping review. *International Journal of Behavioral Medicine, 25,* 17–29.

Sagoe, D., Griffiths, M. D., Erevik, E. K., Høyland, T., Leino, T., Lande, I. A., Sigurdsson, M. E., & Pallesen, S. (2021). Internet-based treatment of gambling problems: A systematic review and meta-analysis of randomized controlled trials. *Journal of Behavioral Addictions, 10,* 546–565.

Salamanca-Sanabria, A., Richards, D., & Timulak, L. (2019). Adapting an internet-delivered intervention for depression for a Colombian college student population: An illustration of an integrative empirical approach. *Internet Interventions, 15,* 76–86.

Schneider, L. H., Hadjistavropoulos, H. D., & Faller, Y. N. (2016). Internet-delivered cognitive behaviour therapy for depressive symptoms: An exploratory examination of therapist behaviours and their relationship to outcome and therapeutic alliance. *Behavioural and Cognitive Psychotherapy, 44,* 625–639.

Schoenenberg, K., & Martin, A. (2024). Empathy, working alliance, treatment expectancy and credibility in video and face-to-face psychotherapeutic first contact. *Psychotherapy Research34,* 626637

Schønning, A., & Nordgreen, T. (2021). Predicting treatment outcomes in guided internet-delivered therapy for anxiety disorders – The role of treatment self-efficacy. *Frontiers in Psychology, 12,* 712421.

Schuster, R., Kaiser, T., Terhorst, Y., Messner, E., Strohmeier, L.-M., & Laireiter, A.-R. (2021). Sample size, sample size planning, and the impact of study context: Systematic review and recommendations by the example of psychological depression treatment. *Psychological Medicine, 51,* 902–908.

Scogin, F., Jamison, C., Floyd, M., & Chaplin, W. F. (1998). Measuring learning in depression treatment: A cognitive bibliotherapy test. *Cognitive Therapy and Research, 22,* 475–482.

Sevilla-Llewellyn-Jones, J., Santesteban-Echarri, O., Pryor, I., McGorry, P., & Alvarez-Jimenez, M. (2018). Web-based mindfulness interventions for mental health treatment: Systematic review and meta-analysis. *JMIR Mental Health*, *5*, e10278.

Shaffer, K. M., Tigershtrom, A., Badr, H., Benvengo, S., Hernandez, M., & Ritterband, L. M. (2020). Dyadic psychosocial eHealth interventions: Systematic scoping review. *Journal of Medical Internet Research*, *22*, e15509.

Shafierizi, S., Faramarzi, M., Nasiri-Amiri, F., Chehrazi, M., Basirat, Z., Kheirkhah, F., & Pasha, H. (2023). Therapist-guided internet-based cognitive behavioral therapy versus face-to-face CBT for depression/anxiety symptoms in infertile women with adjustment disorders: A randomized controlled trial. *Psychotherapy Research*, *33*, 803–819.

Sheehan, D. V., Lecrubier, Y., Sheehan, K. H., Amorim, P., Janavs, J., Weiller, E., Hergueta, T., Baker, R., & Dunbar, G. C. (1998). The Mini-International Neuropsychiatric Interview (M.I.N.I.): The development and validation of a structured diagnostic psychiatric interview for DSM-IV and ICD-10. *Journal of Clinical Psychiatry*, *59*(Suppl 20), 22–33.

Shou, S., Xiu, S., Li, Y., Zhang, N., Yu, J., Ding, J., & Wang, J. (2022). Efficacy of online intervention for ADHD: A meta-analysis and systematic review. *Frontiers in Psychology*, *13*, 854810.

Silfvernagel, K., Gren-Landell, M., Emanuelsson, M., Carlbring, P., & Andersson, G. (2015). Individually tailored internet-based cognitive behavior therapy for adolescents with anxiety disorders: A pilot study. *Internet Interventions*, *2*, 297–302.

Silfvernagel, K., Westlinder, A., Andersson, S., Bergman, K., Hernandez, R. D., Fallhagen, L., Lundqvist, I., Masri, N., Viberg, L., Forsberg, M.-L., Lind, M., Berger, T., Carlbring, P., & Andersson, G. (2018). Individually tailored internet-based cognitive behaviour therapy for older adults with anxiety and depression: A randomised controlled trial. *Cognitive Behaviour Therapy*, *47*, 286–300.

Simon, L., Steinmetz, L., Feige, B., Benz, F., Spiegelhalder, K., & Baumeister, H. (2023). Comparative efficacy of onsite, digital, and other settings for cognitive behavioral therapy for insomnia: A systematic review and network meta-analysis. *Scientific Reports*, *13*, 1929.

REFERENCES

Skivington, K., Matthews, L., Simpson, S. A., Craig, P., Baird, J., Blazeby, J. M., Boyd, K. A., Craig, N., French, D. P., McIntosh, E., Petticrew, M., Rycroft-Malone, J., White, M., & Moore, L. (2021). A new framework for developing and evaluating complex interventions: Update of Medical Research Council guidance. *British Medical Journal, 374*, n2061.

Smoktunowicz, E., Barak, A., Andersson, G., Banos, R. M., Berger, T., Botella, C., Dear, B. F., Donker, T., Ebert, D. D., Hadjistavropoulos, H., Hodgins, D. C., Kaldo, V., Mohr, D. C., Nordgreen, T., Powers, M. B., Riper, H., Ritterband, L. M., Rozental, A., Schueller, S. M., . . . Carlbring, P. (2020). Consensus statement on the problem of terminology in psychological interventions using the internet or digital components. *Internet Interventions, 21*, 100331.

Soucy, J. N., Hadjistavropoulos, H. D., Karin, E., Dear, B. F., & Titov, N. (2021). Brief online motivational interviewing pre-treatment intervention for enhancing internet-delivered cognitive behaviour therapy: A randomized controlled trial. *Internet Interventions, 25*, 100394.

Soucy, J. N., Hadjistavropoulos, H. D., Pugh, N. E., Dear, B. F., & Titov, N. (2019). What are clients asking their therapist during therapist-assisted internet-delivered cognitive behaviour therapy? A content analysis of client questions. *Behavioural and Cognitive Psychotherapy, 47*, 407–420.

Spanhel, K., Balci, S., Feldhahn, F., Bengel, J., Baumeister, H., & Sander, L. B. (2021). Cultural adaptation of internet- and mobile-based interventions for mental disorders: A systematic review. *npj Digital Medicine, 4*, 128.

Spence, S. H., Donovan, C. L., March, S., Gamble, A., Anderson, R. E., Prosser, S., & Kenardy, J. (2011). A randomized controlled trial of online versus clinic-based CBT for adolescent anxiety. *Journal of Consulting Clinical Psychology, 79*, 629–642.

Strandskov, W. S., Ghaderi, A., Andersson, H., Parmskog, N., Hjort, E., Svanberg Wärn, A., Jannert, M., & Andersson, G. (2017). Effects of tailored and ACT-influenced internet-based CBT for eating disorders and the relation between knowledge acquisition and outcome: A randomized controlled trial. *Behavior Therapy, 48*, 624–637.

Strauss, A., & Corbin, J. (1990). *Basics of qualitative research: Grounded theory procedures and techniques*. Sage.

Ström, L., Pettersson, R., & Andersson, G. (2000). A controlled trial of self-help treatment of recurrent headache conducted via the internet. *Journal of Consulting and Clinical Psychology*, *68*, 722–727.

Ström, L., Pettersson, R., & Andersson, G. (2004). Internet-based treatment for insomnia: A controlled evaluation. *Journal of Consulting and Clinical Psychology*, *72*, 113–120.

Svärdman, F., Sjöwall, D., & Lindsäter, E. (2022). Internet-delivered cognitive behavioral interventions to reduce elevated stress: A systematic review and meta-analysis. *Internet Interventions*, *29*, 100553.

Tavares Franquez, R., Del Grossi Moura, M., Cristina Ferreira McClung, D., Barberato-Filho, S., Cruz Lopes, L., Silva, M. T., de Sá Del-Fiol, F., & de Cássia Bergamaschi, C. (2023). E-Health technologies for treatment of depression, anxiety and emotional distress in person with diabetes mellitus: A systematic review and meta-analysis. *Diabetes Research and Clinical Practice*, *203*, 110854.

Tham, A., Jonsson, U., Andersson, G., Söderlund, A., Allard, P., & Bertilsson, G. (2016). Efficacy and tolerability of antidepressants in people aged 65 years or older with major depressive disorder – A systematic review and a meta-analysis. *Journal of Affective Disorders*, *205*, 1–12.

Thorisdottir, A. S., & Asmundson, G. (2022). Internet-delivered cognitive processing therapy for individuals with a history of bullying victimization: A randomized controlled trial. *Cognitive Behaviour Therapy*, *51*, 143–169.

Thornton, L., Batterham, P. J., Fassnacht, D. B., Kay-Lambkin, F., Calear, A. L., & Hunt, S. (2016). Recruiting for health, medical or psychosocial research using Facebook: Systematic review. *Internet Interventions*, *4*, 72–81.

Titov, N., Dear, B., Nielssen, O., Staples, L., Hadjistavropoulos, H., Nugent, M., Adlam, K., Nordgreen, T., Bruvik, K. H., Hovland, A., Repal, A., Mathiasen, K., Kraepelien, M., Blom, K., Svanborg, C., Lindefors, N., & Kaldo, V. (2018). ICBT in routine care: A descriptive analysis of successful clinics in five countries. *Internet Interventions*, *13*, 108–115.

Titov, N., Dear, B. F., Staples, L., Bennett-Levy, J., Klein, B., Rapee, R. M., Andersson, G., Purtell, C., Bezuidenhout, G., & Nielssen, O. B. (2017). The first 30 months of the MindSpot Clinic: Evaluation of a national e-mental health service against project objectives. *Australian and New Zealand Journal of Psychiatry*, *51*, 1227–1239.

Tomasino, K. N., Lattie, E. G., Ho, J., Palac, H. L., Kaiser, S. M., & Mohr, D. C. (2017). Harnessing peer support in an online intervention for older adults with depression. *American Journal of Geriatric Psychiatry*, *25*, 1109–1119.

Topooco, N., Berg, M., Johansson, S., Liljethörn, L., Radvogin, E., Vlaescu, G., Bergman Nordgren, L., Zetterqvist, M., & Andersson, G. (2018). Chat- and internet-based cognitive-behavioural therapy in treatment of adolescent depression: Randomised controlled trial. *BJPsych Open*, *4*, 199–207.

Topooco, N., Riper, H., Araya, R., Berking, M., Brunn, M., Chevreul, K., Cieslak, R., Ebert, D. D., Etchmendy, E., Herrero, R., Kleiboer, A., Krieger, T., García-Palacios, A., Cerga-Pashoja, A., Smoktunowicz, E., Urech, A., Vis, C., Andersson, G., & on behalf of the E-COMPARED Consortium. (2017). Attitudes towards digital treatment for depression: A European stakeholder survey. *Internet Interventions*, *8*, 1–9.

Torous, J., Andersson, G., Bertagnoli, A., Christensen, H., Cuijpers, P., Firth, J., Haim, A., Hsin, H., Hollis, C., Lewis, S., Mohr, D. C., Pratap, A., Roux, S., Sherrill, J., & Arean, P. A. (2019). Towards a consensus around standards for smartphone apps and digital mental health. *World Psychiatry*, *18*, 97–98.

Tulbure, B. T., Andersson, G., Sălăgean, N., Pearce, M. P., & Koenig, H. G. (2018). Religious versus conventional internet-based cognitive behavioral therapy for depression: A randomized controlled trial. *Journal of Religion and Health*, *57*, 1634–1648.

Tulbure, B. T., Szentagotai, A., David, O., Stefan, S., Månsson, K. N. T., David, D., & Andersson, G. (2015). Internet-delivered cognitive-behavioral therapy for social anxiety disorder in Romania: A randomized controlled trial. *PLoS One*, *10*, e0123997.

van Ballegooijen, W., Riper, H., Cuijpers, P., van Oppen, P., & Smit, J. H. (2016). Validation of online psychometric instruments for common mental health disorders: A systematic review. *BMC Psychiatry*, *16*, 45.

van der Vaart, R., Witting, M., Riper, H., Kooistra, L., Bohlmeijer, E. T., & van Gemert-Pijnen, L. J. (2014). Blending online therapy into regular face-to-face therapy for depression: Content, ratio and preconditions according to patients and therapists using a Delphi study. *BMC Psychiatry*, *14*, 355.

Vigerland, S., Lenhard, F., Bonnert, M., Lalouni, M., Hedman, E., Ahlen, J., Olen, O., Serlachius, E., & Ljotsson, B. (2016). Internet-delivered cognitive behavior therapy for children and adolescents: A systematic review and meta-analysis. *Clinical Psychology Review*, *50*, 1–10.

Vigerland, S., Ljótsson, B., Thulin, U., Öst, L.-G., Andersson, G., & Serlachius, E. (2016). Internet-delivered cognitive behavioral therapy for children with anxiety disorders: A randomized controlled trial. *Behaviour Research and Therapy*, *76*, 47–56.

Vlaescu, G., Alasjö, A., Miloff, A., Carlbring, P., & Andersson, G. (2016). Features and functionality of the Iterapi platform for internet-based psychological treatment. *Internet Interventions*, *6*, 107–114.

Vlaescu, G., Carlbring, P., & Andersson, G. (2024). Features and functionality of the Iterapi platform for internet-based psychological treatment – An update. Unpublished manuscript.

Watkins, E. R., & Newbold, A. (2020). Factorial designs help to understand how psychological therapy works. *Frontiers in Psychiatry*, *11*, 429.

Watkins, E. R., Newbold, A., Tester-Jones, M., Collins, L. M., & Mostazir, M. (2023). Investigation of active ingredients within internet-delivered cognitive behavioral therapy for depression: A randomized optimization trial. *JAMA Psychiatry*, *80*, 942–951.

Watkins, P. L., & Clum, G. A. (Eds.). (2008). *Handbook of self-help therapies*. Routledge.

Webb, T. L., Joseph, J., Yardley, L., & Michie, S. (2010). Using the Internet to promote health behavior change: A systematic review and meta-analysis of the impact of theoretical basis, use of behavior change techniques, and mode of delivery on efficacy. *Journal of Medical Internet Research*, *12*, e4.

Wells, A. (2009). *Metacognitive therapy for anxiety and depression*. New York: Guilford Press.

White, V., Linardon, J., Stone, J. E., Holmes-Truscott, E., Olive, L., Mikocka-Walus, A., Hendrieckx, C., Evans, S., & Speight, J. (2022). Online psychological interventions to reduce symptoms of depression, anxiety, and general distress in those with chronic health conditions:

A systematic review and meta-analysis of randomized controlled trials. *Psychological Medicine*, *52*, 548–573.

Wind, T. R., Rijkeboer, M., Andersson, G., & Riper, H. (2020). The COVID-19 pandemic: The 'black swan' for mental health care and a turning point for e-health. *Internet Interventions*, *20*, 100317.

Wu, Y., Fenfen, E., Wang, Y., Xu, M., Liu, S., Zhou, L., Song, G., Shang, X., Yang, C., Yang, K., & Li, X. (2023). Efficacy of internet-based cognitive-behavioral therapy for depression in adolescents: A systematic review and meta-analysis. *Internet Interventions*, *34*, 100673.

Xiang, X., Wu, S., Zuverink, A., Tomasino, K. N., An, R., & Himle, J. A. (2020). Internet-delivered cognitive behavioral therapies for late-life depressive symptoms: A systematic review and meta-analysis. *Aging & Mental Health*, *24*, 1196–1206.

Yardley, L., Morrison, L., Bradbury, K., & Muller, I. (2015). The person-based approach to intervention development: application to digital health-related behavior change interventions. *Journal of Medical Internet Research*, *17*, e30.

Zalaznik, D., Strauss, A. Y., Halaj, A., Barzilay, S., Fradkin, I., Katz, B. A., Ganor, T., Ebert, D. D., Andersson, G., & Huppert, J. D. (2021). Patient alliance with the program predicts treatment outcomes whereas alliance with the therapist predicts adherence in internet-based therapy for panic disorder. *Psychotherapy Research*, *31*, 1022–1035.

Zale, A., Lasecke, M., Baeza-Hernandez, K., Testerman, A., Aghakhani, S., Muñoz, R. F., & Bunge, E. L. (2021). Technology and psychotherapeutic interventions: Bibliometric analysis of the past four decades. *Internet Interventions*, *25*, 100425.

Zarski, A. C., Velten, J., Knauer, J., Berking, M., & Ebert, D. D. (2022). Internet- and mobile-based psychological interventions for sexual dysfunctions: A systematic review and meta-analysis. *npj Digital Medicine*, *5*, 139.

Zetterqvist, K., Maanmies, J., Ström, L., & Andersson, G. (2003). Randomized controlled trial of internet-based stress management. *Cognitive Behaviour Therapy*, *3*, 151–160.

Zhang, Y., Flannery, M., Zhang, Z., Underhill-Blazey, M., Bobry, M., Leblanc, N., Rodriguez, D., & Zhang, C. (2024). Digital health psychosocial intervention in adult patients with cancer and their families: Systematic review and meta-analysis. *JMIR Cancer*, *10*, e46116.

Zuelke, A. E., Luppa, M., Löbner, M., Pabst, A., Schlapke, C., Stein, J., & Riedel-Heller, S. G. (2021). Effectiveness and feasibility of Internet-based interventions for grief after bereavement: Systematic review and meta-analysis. *JMIR Mental Health*, *8*, e29661.

Index

For Product Safety Concerns and Information please contact our EU representative GPSR@taylorandfrancis.com Taylor & Francis Verlag GmbH, Kaufingerstraße 24, 80331 München, Germany

Printed and bound by CPI Group (UK) Ltd, Croydon, CR0 4YY
08/06/2025
01897000-0001